D0394241

Unthinking

The Surprising Forces Behind What We Buy

HARRY BECKWITH

**BUSINESS
PLUS**

NEW YORK   BOSTON

Business Plus
Hachette Book Group
237 Park Avenue
New York, NY 10017

www.HachetteBookGroup.com

Business Plus is an imprint of Grand Central Publishing.
The Business Plus name and logo are trademarks of Hachette Book Group, Inc.

Printed in the United States of America

First Edition: January 2011

10 9 8 7 6 5 4 3 2 1

Library of Congress Cataloging-in-Publication Data

Beckwith, Harry
   Unthinking : the surprising forces behind what we buy / Harry Beckwith.—1st ed.
      p. cm.
   Includes index.
   ISBN 978-0-446-56414-4
   1. Consumer behavior.   2. Consumption (Economics)—Psychological aspects.   3. Marketing—Psychological aspects.   I. Title.

   HF5415.32.B435 2011
   658.8'342–dc22

                                                                2010017185

To Harry, Will,
Cole, and Cooper

Contents

Contents

Welcome.

This is a story about our planet's most fascinating subject: us. It's about us and what leads us to choose what we choose, without really thinking. You can find the forces that influence our choices in several places. This book looks into three—our childhoods, our culture, and our eyes—where we find dozens of surprising stories. They range from the birth of the iPhone to the death of a sex symbol; from the fall of *The Mary Tyler Moore Show* to the rise of the Nintendo Wii; and from the heights of George Clooney and Regis Philbin to the lengths of the titles of our current best sellers.

Throughout the book, we spotlight the masters of modern marketing and how they tap these forces to influence our choices, ranging from the perfect bleach for our cottons to the best person to check our teeth.

Which leads us first to one of the oddest cases of all: the very strange case of Kobe Bryant.

DECIDING WITHOUT THINKING

The Very Strange Case of Kobe Bryant

In February 2009, the editors of *Sports Illustrated* asked the players in the National Basketball Association a question to which the editors already knew the answer: "With a game on the line—where one shot will win or lose it—which player would you choose to take the last shot?"

Every basketball fan can guess the players' answer: Kobe Bryant, the handsome veteran All Star shooting guard of the world-champion Los Angeles Lakers. The voting wasn't close; 76 percent of the players chose Bryant. In a tie for a remote second place, Denver's Chauncey Billups, Boston's Paul Pierce, and Cleveland's LeBron James each won just 3 percent of the votes.

Like basketball fans, Kobe's NBA colleagues had seen ESPN's highlights for years, which included over a dozen clips of Bryant making game-winning shots. In "crunch time," as fans call these final moments, Kobe's chiseled face conveys that any resistance to him will be futile. That's why fans and players often repeat, "Kobe is *the Man*."

So Kobe was the expected choice, the logical

choice, the overwhelming choice; he received more than twenty-five times more votes than each of the three runners-up. There was just one problem:

It was a horrible choice.

We know this because in the 2003–2004 season, 82games.com started tracking these last-minute shots. Their computations showed that between the start of the 2003–2004 season and the time of the *Sports Illustrated* poll, Kobe had made fourteen last-minute shots. That's a lot—more than two shots per season—but three players had made more, most notably James, who had made seventeen.

But the problem with the players' choice wasn't that Kobe doesn't make these shots. He does. But as skilled as he is at making them, at that point he'd proven even more adept at missing them. He'd missed forty-two: 75 percent of his shots!

For perspective, compare Bryant's numbers with those of Carmelo Anthony, the 6-foot-8-inch small forward for the Denver Nuggets. Kobe Bryant looks like a stone killer at crunch time, but Anthony plays like one. In "clutch" situations in the 2008–2009 season—with a game in the last five minutes or in overtime, with neither team having more than a five-point lead—Anthony made 56.5 percent of his shots. Bryant made 45.7 percent.

On three-point attempts, Anthony performed even better, making an amazing 58.5 percent of these attempts, compared to Bryant's 40 percent. (The league's season record for the three-point percentage is 52.4 percent.)

And on game-winning shot attempts with fewer than twenty-four seconds remaining, how did Anthony fare? Again, "Melo" was mellow: 48.1 percent—almost twice Kobe's 25 percent.

Despite what most NBA players thought they'd seen and believed they knew, Kobe Bryant is not a great last-minute shooter. He's not even an average player in these situations; the NBA last-minute shot average is 29.8 percent. Had Kobe been merely average, the Lakers would have won two more games over that stretch. Had Kobe possessed Anthony's gift in these situations, the Lakers could have won as many as twenty-three additional games—*almost three more wins per year.*

The players hardly could have made a worse choice. Several NBA players had made at least half of their last-minute shots at the time of voting, and Travis Outlaw of the Portland Trail Blazers had made six out of seven.

Which raises the question: *Could* the NBA players have made a *worse* choice?

Yes. One.

The players could have chosen the player who, on thirty-seven last-minute shots, had made just six, a woeful 16.2 percent, for the worst record in the league. Now *that* guy is absolutely the last NBA player you would want to take a last-minute shot. Whatever you do, do not choose him. Give the ball to anyone else. If you can't think of anyone else, shoot the ball yourself.

And that man's name? It's Chauncey Billups—*the man who got the second-most votes in this poll.*

How could these players, with their night-to-night, eighty-two regular-season games a year, and weeks and weeks of playoffs, and all the knowledge that comes with that, make two such bad choices? And this is the best answer:

These players are just like us.

All of us quickly learn rules of thumb—shortcuts for making decisions that psychologists call heuristics. We learn and use them because we must; we don't have the time to ponder every decision. And one of our favorite heuristics is stereotyping: Older is wiser, accountants are analytical, and huge animals aren't agile. The NBA players were doing what we do every day: They were shortcutting.

Let's see how.

To understand the players' unthinking, look at the phrase that describes Kobe Bryant: "the world-champion Los Angeles Lakers' handsome veteran All Star shooting guard."

Because of their years of title-winning success (only the Boston Celtics have won more NBA championships) and their position in the nation's second-largest media market, the Lakers appear on television more often than any other team. Television executives know there aren't enough viewers in Carmelo Anthony's Denver—or in Outlaw's then-home of Portland—to justify covering those teams when there are so many more viewers in New York, Chicago, and Los Angeles. So for every time that Anthony's Nuggets appear on national television, Bryant's Lakers appear five times.

As a result, Kobe has the most often seen face in professional basketball; he's familiar. And as we will see throughout this book, we humans are unusually biased toward choosing things that seem familiar.

To make Kobe even more familiar to fans and players, Kobe is a *veteran*. At the time of the NBA poll, Kobe was midway through his thirteenth NBA season, having skipped college and gone straight to the NBA in 1996. Anthony and James were just in their sixth seasons, relative new kids. That longevity made Kobe even more familiar.

In addition, when we hear "veteran," we make other favorable assumptions about a player; we stereotype. We call veterans "cool" and often "wily." We think veterans have acquired the emotional makeup to withstand late-game pressure and the cleverness, based on their many years of play, to find some way to get the ball into the basket. So we want a veteran shooting a last-minute shot—a thirteen-year veteran like Kobe.

And lo and behold, if Kobe isn't available, then the NBA players want twelve-year veteran Chauncey Billups, the NBA's worst last-minute shooter, to take the shot instead.

Two other words gave the players a shortcut to deciding. Basketball is played with five players on a team, each with specific roles with specific names.

First, there are the centers. They usually stand about 7 feet tall and are most skilled at retrieving missed shots and making shots near the basket. Centers are rarely good long-distance shooters, in part because it's foolish to practice 20-foot shots when you can perfect slamming the ball through the hoop from inches away.

So you don't want a center taking a last-minute shot. He's not prepared.

A basketball team also sports two forwards. One is bigger and stronger and called the power forward. The other is smaller and faster and called the small forward.

That leaves two more players: the guards. The first directs the offense, which is why he's called the point guard.

That's four players, and it doesn't sound like you

want any of them shooting a last-minute shot. Centers aren't good shooters, big guys lack finesse, small guys are small, and point guards direct the offense but aren't usually known for their shooting.

Fortunately, the final position sounds ideal for taking this last-minute shot. This player's primary role is to shoot, often from a distance, which forces defensive players to come out to stop him. He's called the shooting guard, and—as you knew or just guessed—that's Kobe Bryant's position.

You do want the *shooting* guard shooting your last shot, don't you? Especially the *twelve-time All Star* shooting guard—wouldn't he be the best shooter in the league?

Another force that biased the players' choice is one that biases all of our choices: money. We consistently take price as a quality signal; the higher the price, the higher the perceived quality. In 2009, Kobe's salary from the Lakers was $23,034,375, a total surpassed only by the $23,329,561 earned by the Houston Rockets' Tracy McGrady, who had been injured for three months when the editors polled the players.

One final element may have influenced the players' choice: Kobe's face. It's beautiful; *People* magazine has featured Kobe twice in its annual "50 Most Beautiful People" issue. Looks tricks us, repeatedly, in ways we will explore. We think attractive people are more intelligent, honest, and emotionally sound—better than average at almost everything. Other things being nearly equal, we want the beautiful person to make the presentation, land our plane in Minneapolis, and take the last shot.

Now, many Americans react to this entire argument in a typical American way, insisting, "There are lies, damn lies, and statistics." They see statistics like Kobe Bryant's ugly 25-percent performance on last-minute shots and respond, "I don't care what the numbers might say. You can prove anything with statistics."

That's not true.

There are many things you cannot prove with statistics. You cannot prove that it's safer to drive 95 miles an hour than to drive 60; you cannot prove that New York Decembers are warmer than New York Augusts; and you cannot prove that Kobe Bryant is a good choice for making a last-minute shot—*unless your only other choice is Chauncey Billups.*

But you can prove that every day, we make odd choices like the NBA players did in this case. Why? Shortcutting is one answer, and the second lurks deep in each of us. Within the last five years, I've been inside two Fortune 100 companies that made critical decisions: choosing a provider for a massive outsourcing contract in the first case and picking a new investment bank in the second. In each case, the companies' decision makers tried to assemble all the facts but still couldn't decide; something was missing. So they made unannounced visits to their finalists' headquarters, felt the pulse, got a feeling, then flew home and chose their firms. How did all of them explain their final choice?

"It just felt right."

That's the rule, not the exception. When our shortcuts don't work, we decide with our feelings, usually within seconds, then reassemble the facts to support our decision. So what are these feelings that lead us to choose what we choose?

An important force that explains the players' choice is fear. We deeply fear looking and feeling foolish. Like all those corporate purchasing agents in the 1980s who knew the axiom that "no one ever got fired for choosing IBM," the NBA players knew they'd never look foolish for choosing Kobe. Even if Kobe missed, they and everyone else still would think they'd made the right choice.

This book examines three major influences that drive our feelings—our childhoods, our American culture, and our eyes—and it's to those influences, and some of the most remarkable stories I have ever heard, that we now turn.

THE FORCES AND THEIR SOURCES

1. OUR CHILDHOODS

I. Our Love of Play

——

If you have not seen it, go now.

(A spoiler alert: Several of your days will be made if you go to www.ted.com and enter "polar bear" and "Stuart Brown" in its search box. So go there now and return, or continue, knowing that the spoiler follows.)

On the video, you see a photo of a polar bear approaching a Siberian husky in Manitoba, Canada. The 1,200-pound bear's predatory stare makes it clear: The husky is lunch. Then you notice the husky's body language, which tells you he sees a different opportunity. The dog is bowing, with his tail wagging, sending a message that every dog owner recognizes: Let's play!

The bear rises up, its claws retracted, opening itself to the husky. The two then come together and begin an unforgettable ballet. They nuzzle and wrestle like mother and puppy; they play. In one particularly endearing photo, you see in the barely open eyes of the bear its bliss and a reminder of why we play: for the sheer delight.

Dr. Stuart Brown, who presented these photos at the May 2008 Art Center Design Conference in Pasadena, California, is among the researchers who have concluded that animals, including us, are programmed to play; we need it to develop normally. Play-deprived adults often develop antisocial personalities, and play-deprived rats die.

Puppies and dogs, bears and cubs, babies and adults—play is basic to us.

Years ago, this discovery led a historian named Johan Huizinga to offer that we should not be called *Homo sapiens,* literally "wise men," after all. We should be called *Homo ludens*: man the player.

Our enterprises regularly overlook this. They treat us like their vision of polar bears: serious, acquisitive, predatory. As we will see in what follows, today's shrewdest marketers see us as the bears and huskies that we really are: animals enchanted by play.

All Play, Some Work

Just watch everyone and anyone, all day long.

Before work each day, most men read news

about play: the sports page. (Most younger men read it online the night before.) Well before lunch, millions recheck the performance of their fantasy teams or post on Internet fan boards about their Lions, Tigers, or Bears.

At breaks in office halls, they replay Saturday's and Sunday's games and second-guess the coaches. Not long afterwards, they close their office doors to search for tickets for the next weekend's game. When they succeed, they don't say that they "got" tickets or "found" them. No, they "scored" some tickets. They won.

Of course they did; in America, even getting tickets to the game is a game.

When we finally get down to work, we play. We don't add a client; we "win" the account. Or we won it while fishing for it, as our language suggests again: We "landed" the account.

Asked about their apparent lust for business, the very successful insist that it's not about money. "Money," they assure us and remind themselves, "is just a way of keeping score." Money is the trophy; work is the game.

On our way home, we stop at a store, decide we feel lucky, and buy lottery tickets; we buy them in numbers beyond comprehension. In 2008, Target, State Farm Insurance, and Microsoft each earned more than $60 billion in revenue, but their successes paled in comparison to state lotteries, which swallowed over $77 billion. If these lotteries merged tonight into a corporation, tomorrow they'd be America's twenty-second-largest company and the world's seventy-first-largest company.

Sex, another of our favorite activities, is all play. That thinking starts from the day we start thinking about sex. Boys "get to second base," then third. Then, like the football player racing to the end zone, they "go all the way" or "score." How does all this fun begin? With play, of course: fore*play*.

Later in life, we call the sexually active man, whom we once called a playboy, a player. Sex is play.

The player marries and settles down. Too often, after kids and seven-year itches come and counseling fails, the marriage implodes. If the man has scored well in business, he goes trolling for his next wife and finds one. But the new young blonde isn't merely a new wife; she's a medal. She's a "trophy" wife.

Of course, men don't pursue sex constantly, but tens of millions still are in their bedrooms right now, as parents know too well. When these young men are not sleeping, often until well after lunch, they are entranced by their aptly named closest friend: a *Play*Station.

Even renting hotel rooms and purchasing airplane tickets have become games, as Priceline has cleverly recognized. We go on Priceline and enter an auction to score the best price. Priceline lets us know we won; it even announces our victory with exclamation points.

All work and no play? Does that person exist? We play all day. And the best marketers recognize the depth of our desire and answer it, in everything from cell phones to investment firms.

eBay and Our Other Toys

Consider the phone that changed the mobile device business, Apple's iPhone. Study its screen for five seconds, and then ask, "Where have I seen those colors before?"

It's hard to miss what those colors are telling us. *They're the bright primary colors of our childhood toys.*

The iPhone screen uses the same colors used by the Fisher-Price toys of our childhoods: lime green, aqua, Trix cereal red, Cheerios box yellow, Kix box orange. The symbols in the icons? Simple and playful.

Look at the iPhone icon for "Messages" as one example. What is that and where did you first see it?

Of course: you saw it in the comic books you first read as a child. The "Message" symbol is a word balloon, white on Trix cereal's lime green.

Look at the color of the phone's iPod symbol, then at the Fisher-Price website, and you'll see it: the cheery orange color for Fisher-Price Babygear. The purple used for the iTunes symbol and the blue for its email symbol? That's the Fisher-Price "Shop" purple and "Games & Activities" blue.

"All that distinguishes men from boys," we've heard, "is the price of their toys." The iPod shouts this, with the colors that call us back to our childhood: *I am a toy.*

Apple promised that from its inception. It told us that it wasn't a computer, but an Apple, like the one we once tried to bribe our teachers with.

Ben & Jerry play with us, wrapping their ice cream cartons in cartoons and their ice cream names in puns, like Cherry Garcia. The next time you pass by a Jamba Juice, stop in and look at the signs: cartoon oranges, cartoon typography, Fisher-Price toy colors. Jamba Juice gets us: We are kids who love to play. The cartoon logo beckoning us in to the playfully named Noodles & Company and T.G.I. Friday's and its waitstaff wearing their "flair" promise the same thing. We play with our food.

The Mini Cooper keeps alive the tradition started by the Volkswagen bug: car as toy. The animation wizards at Pixar studios saw this, too: Their Luigi character in their movie *Cars* looks like the Mini Cooper's sillier brother. But dozens of cars appeal to our love of play, as their category makes clear: they're *sports* cars.

Costco's appeal is to our love of play; its strategy actually borrows the name of a 1950's children's board game, Treasure Hunt. A trip to Costco is an adult *Where's Waldo?* adventure: Might we find fine French Bordeaux for $12 a bottle? Cashmere scarves for $10? Just what might be around the next corner?

Costco is shopping as play.

Venture onto eBay, and you see a button that reads "Buy It Now." A true bargain seeker always would hit this button, because it guarantees the item's relatively low price. But in 2007, a University of California, Berkeley, economist named Ulrike M. Malmendier started studying eBay customers and found something unexpected: Most of them ignored the Buy It Now option. They chose to enter the auction instead, where they ended up paying more. They wanted more than the item; they wanted the game of the auction.

For a reverse auction, there's BoltBus. Play its game right, and you can be the first to book the March 1 trip from New York to Boston for their starting price: $1. "Bolt for a Buck" works, backed by little conventional advertising.

eBay and Bolt are play.

The name Yahoo promises us play. It proclaims it is not a search engine or directory but a toy so fun it will make us shout, "Yahoo!"

Google says that to us, too, partly by stealing Yahoo's clever use of the beloved-from-childhood double-o sound. Consider all these "oo" words and their playfulness: kaboom, boob, kook, boonies, goofy, doofus, kazoo, Goonies, Goofy, Kool-Aid, Froot Loops, Looney Tunes, Dr. Seuss and his Cindy Lou Who, Yogi Bear's sidekick Boo-Boo, Scooby-Doo, and, not incidentally or accidentally, YouTube, a double-double "oo" sound meant to suggest to us "really fun to watch videos."

Then there's Pamela Skaist-Levy and Gela Nash-Taylor. In 1996, they started a line of women's clothes with a name that manages to rhyme the playful "oo" sounds while playing on sex as play: Juicy Couture, most famous for its velour sweatpants with "Juicy" scrawled across the butt.

In 2010, BMW called out to our playful inner child. "Joy seeks out the kid in all of us," the ad for its sporty 3 Series car assures us, below the photo of a khakis-and-polo-clad, gray-haired man. You're never too old to be young, they assure us. "At BMW, we don't make cars. We make joy."

Our kitchens call out to the kids in us, too. Specialty shops like Williams-Sonoma look more and more like toy shops. With Cuisinart and Le Creuset leading the way, you can choose pots, spatulas, whisks, pastry brushes, ice cream makers, immersion blenders, and hand mixers in an assortment of toy colors, including Cuisinart's Fisher-Price palette with iMac names: Pomegranate, Parsley, Tangerine, Buttercup, and a playful purple called Crush. Nearby, the playfully named Pop Ware offers cooking's most mundane items, strainers and colanders, in toy colors: Bright Red, Bright Blue, and Lime Green. Today, we can feel playful while draining water off our spaghetti noodles.

In 2010, a huge buzz and over $8 million in venture capital funding surrounded the website Polyvore. The bright idea behind it was that women would welcome the mix-and-match clothes and accessories from different sites and create new looks from them. It's easy to understand the site's appeal. Isn't it simply an electronic version of a favorite girls' play activity of decades ago—paper dolls—and a grownup version of dressing Barbie?

Today's great marketers ask the question: "Should we add an element of play here—and if not, why not?" Several manufacturers are asking that right now. They looked at their iPhones and asked, "What if our washing machine looked and felt like that and made doing laundry more fun?"

Let's play, we say, and generations of us make it into a cult a film about never growing up, *The Big Lebowski*. The hero, known as "The Dude"—naturally capturing that "oo" sound of play—refuses to grow up, and audiences love him.

And he's not alone, as we will see next.

Fridays at Maine South:
Forever Young

Drive east from Chicago's O'Hare Airport to a remarkable monument to the role of play in our culture: the home football field of the Maine South Hawks, regularly among Illinois' best high school teams and many times its state champion. The school is also the alma mater of Hillary Clinton.

The playing field itself testifies to the central role of play in twenty-first-century American culture: It cost $1.2 million to install in 2008 and looks every penny of it, with an enormous red hawk artfully rendered in the middle of the field and the school name and nickname rendered in massive red letters in each end zone.

We live in a country so devoted to play—some might argue obsessed—that our high school football fields cost over $1 million, and Park Ridge's elected officials worry very little that the outlay will cost them the next election.

But there's more testament to our childlike love of play than the Maine South field and the play on it. Look into the stands, and notice how the girls are dressed. They sport the Park Ridge uniform: tight blue jeans, snug sweaters, lots of eye makeup, and what appears to be a Maine South dress code mandate: a pair of Uggs in any of many colors.

But look again.

Sometimes that was a Maine South student who walked by you. But if you had looked closer, you would have noticed far more wrinkles than you see on teenage girls, although the wrinkles are well concealed. That wasn't a student you noticed. It was a student's mom.

At Maine South on a Friday night, as at other schools on other Friday nights all across America, you cannot tell the mothers from the daughters by their clothing. The adults copy the children, right down to dieting to maintain the illusion of youth and the white blouses peeking out from bottoms of sweaters. Obviously, the moms' efforts sometimes work; they got at least one author's attention.

But it's hard to escape another conclusion while watching boys play this night in October just north of Chicago: We are still children, craving to be children, buying the more expensive toys that allow us to play and even remind us, as an iPhone does, of the colors of childhood while we sport the clothes that make us feel—as expressed in the words of the Boomers' poet laureate, Bob Dylan— that we can stay forever young.

II. Our Love of Surprise

—

"Chasing Pavements" Up "Solsbury Hill": How Music Gets Us

When you heard Judy Garland sing the first word, "Some...where," in "Over the Rainbow" in *The Wizard of Oz,* it happened to you.

The first time most people hear "As Tears Go By" by the Rolling Stones, "Superstition" by Stevie Wonder, "Solsbury Hill" by Peter Gabriel, any song by Joni Mitchell, Kim Carnes, or Adele, and the memorable long opening twang of the Beatles' "A Hard Day's Night," it happens again.

Clever music students might be able to explain what caused each of those reactions—except the last.

Garland's first two notes, "Some...where," leap a full octave. That's rare, especially from a twelve-year old girl.

In "As Tears Go By," the surprise is hearing a guitar-driven hard rock group like the Stones singing to the accompaniment of—of all possible instruments—classical violins. (Similarly, there is the incongruity of the Stones' aggressive lyrics in "Under My Thumb," heard over a signature instrument of jazz, the gentle vibes.)

In "Superstition," our surprise comes from the unusual collection of notes; Wonder plays almost the entire song on the black keys. (Don't try that at home.)

In "Solsbury Hill," what surprises us is hearing a rock song and bracing for rock's signature 4/4 beat, and hearing instead a song in 7/4 time, a beat unusual in most music. (Notable exceptions would include Pink Floyd's "Money" and part of the chorus in the Beatles' "All You Need Is Love.")

Hearing Joni Mitchell surprises us because she tunes her guitar erratically, creating notes different from any we've heard before.

And no musical training is required to realize the surprise of hearing Kim Carnes and Adele. Their voices remind us less of humans and more of forces of nature. Listening to Adele, we experience the added surprise of hearing, in "Chasing Pavements," the longest vowels in popular music.

Then there's the opening twang of "Hard Day's Night," for over forty years one of music's great mysteries.

How did the Beatles do that?

For almost forty-six years, musicians tried to duplicate that opening chord by combining a Rickenbacker twelve-string guitar like George Harrison's with John Lennon's six-string and Paul McCartney's bass. Everyone failed; they couldn't make the sound. Then in 2010 a mathematician, of all people, took a shot. Instead of grabbing three guitars, he grabbed a yellow pad and felt pen and performed a calculation called a Fourier transform. From it, he deduced that a fourth instrument was involved, likely played by the Beatles' composer, George Martin: a piano striking an F note.

But that opening note was so surprising and without precedent that it took over forty-five years, and a formula that includes the sequence $f(x)e^{-2\Pi ix\Sigma}$, to explain it.

In classical music, the composer establishes the tone of the piece with what's called the tonic note. Then for the rest of the song, the composer dances around the note without ever returning to it—variations of the note but never the note itself—until the final resolution. Instinctively, our brain wonders: How will this song return to its tonic note?

What we feel in the meantime is the delight of the journey, the surprise notes and rhythms, and then our pleasure when, like a riddle, the music resolves itself by returning to the tonic note.

The music we love depends on surprise. If a song falls into a predictable pattern, we lose all interest. It's the surprises—the notes or lyrics we do not expect—that make a piece creep into the soul.

Our brains love surprises. We grew up wanting Cracker Jack for the "surprise in every package." As teenagers we started to crave horror films, which leapt beyond surprise and into shocking. We crave surprise endings in movies and exclaim about predictable ones. We complain whenever life seems like just one thing after another; we want surprise.

We love joy, and joy depends entirely on surprise. If we know something will happen, it barely pleases us. The moments that delight us—the experiences that we love—take us by surprise.

Quentin Tarantino's audacious 2009 movie *Inglourious Basterds* begins as a classic heroic-Americans-versus-demonic-Nazis movie and never visits there again.

To fit the mold, the Nazi colonel should look and behave brutishly. But in an Oscar-winning performance, German actor Christoph Waltz plays him as so dainty and polite that he gently asks a

Frenchman whom he suspects of harboring Jews, "Might we switch from French to English?"

When a Jewish woman flees the house, the Nazi colonel spots her, draws out his pistol, takes aim, and—surprise—lets her escape down the grassy field.

The Nazis in *Basterds* kill only at a distance, sniping in kill-or-be-killed scenes. Our American heroes, by contrast to all film convention, scalp every victim and carve deep swastika tattoos into the survivors' foreheads.

We feel certain that the woman who escaped, Shosanna, will survive to avenge the Nazis' slaughter of her family. She does. But almost the instant she does, she feels love toward the Nazi war hero whom she shoots, and she tries to turn him over to save his life.

We love surprises and remember them—which is what gives them such marketing force. Surprises stick in our minds, like the surprises in this film that this author remembers more than six months after seeing it.

We see the force of surprise again in jokes. The effectiveness of a joke depends entirely on surprise, too, as Aristotle, among others, said long ago. There's the setup, followed by a surprising twist.

The conclusion has to surprise us; if we can guess the punch line before we hear it, the joke fails.

Hence *"I slept like a baby. I cried all night."*

The setup makes us expect a quiet night's sleep. Then we hear the opposite. That's surprising, and that's what makes it funny.

Many readers have heard about the grasshopper who walks into a bar, sits down, and asks what drink the bartender would recommend. The bartender says the grasshopper is in for a surprise: There's a drink named for him! We know, or expect, that there is a cocktail called a grasshopper.

The grasshopper responds, "There's a drink called *Mervin*?" The surprise of hearing "Mervin" instead of "grasshopper" makes us laugh.

Jokes are rooted in the power of surprise—something we crave from childhood.

Riddles & Rhymes & Theming Lines

"She drives me crazy, oh yeah
Like no else.
She drives me crazy
And I can't help myself."

The name of the band flashes instantly in a million minds: Fine Young Cannibals!

Why do we remember Fine Young Cannibals twenty years after their last hit but forget the name of products just minutes after hearing and seeing those names six times in a commercial?

It's not because the Cannibals endured. They were two-hit wonders who enjoyed fifteen weeks of fame in 1989, then disbanded less than three years later.

Why do we remember that name?

Because just as Coldplay riddles us with "How can play be cold?" and 50 Cent makes us wonder "Shouldn't it be *cents*?" the group's name makes us wonder: How can people who eat people possibly be fine? Our minds demand a resolution of that riddle; we insist on closure and hate loose ends. (That's why collectibles thrive. Once we buy a couple items, the plea "Be sure to get the whole set!" tantalizes us into doing just that.)

The word "Yahoo" sounds familiar; it's just surprising when applied to a tech service or product, just as Apple is a familiar term when describing a fruit but surprising when describing a computer. "Buffalo" and "Springfield" are familiar names when describing towns in New York and Illinois but surprising when combined to describe a rock group. Their names are riddles.

Names like "Buffalo Springfield" sounded even more surprising in that group's heyday, because before them, music groups had always used plural names: The Temptations and The Supremes, or The Four Tops and The Dave Clark Five.

Then along came Jefferson Airplane and Buffalo Springfield, which startled us. Four or five people singing but with a *singular* name?

To see riddles at work in marketing, consider the following:

Put a tiger in your tank. (Enco)
The future is bright. The future is Orange.
    (Orange Telecom)
So good, cats ask for it by name. (Meow Mix)
Say it with flowers. (FTD)

Each of these marketing slogans has won a spot in the Advertising Slogan Hall of Fame. (Yes, we have halls of fame for everything.)

What do they share in common?

Each is a riddle, because each suggests something impossible. A tiger cannot squeeze into a gas tank, the future isn't a color, and neither cats nor tulips can talk. Each slogan suggests one of the great riddles: How do you do something that sounds impossible?

Now consider:

Sometimes you feel like a nut, sometimes you
    don't. (Peter Paul Mounds Bar)
When it rains, it pours. (Morton Salt)
The Citi never sleeps. (Citibank)
Nothing runs like a Deere. (John Deere)
Capitalist tool (Forbes)
Think small. (Volkswagen)
Heinz meanz beanz. (Heinz)

Each of these slogans takes a familiar phrase or
image and adds a twist. The familiar expression "I
feel like a nut" means that you feel slightly crazy.
Hershey's gave this surprise twist: Whether you feel
like *having* a nut or you don't, buy a Mounds Bar,
because they come with nuts or without.

When Morton Salt manufactured the first salt that
wouldn't clump in moist air, they took a familiar
phrase but cleverly put it in a new context: Morton
Salt still pours even when it's wet outside.

New York was famous as "the city that never
sleeps." Citibank gave the phrase new meaning as the
bank that tried harder: "The *Citi* that never sleeps."

Deere twisted the phrase "He runs like deer" to
tell us that nothing runs like a John Deere; there's
also a wonderful element of play here in the puns
on "runs" and "deer."

In the 1960s and '70s, hippies labeled those who
they considered sellouts to American business as

"capitalist tools." In clever retaliation, *Forbes* proudly embraced the phrase and twisted it, proclaiming itself as the representative of that system and a vital tool for business.

"Think Small" flipped a classic American expression of optimism, "Think big," and told us it was time we considered an automobile so small they called it "the bug," the charming underdog of its era.

Heinz riffed on the familiar phrase "It doesn't mean beans to me" to give the company a foothold in the canned beans market.

Why do marketers spend so much time worrying about these little phrases? It's largely because a message needs to have an emotional peak and because the brain's processing power is limited, particularly when it involves something that minimally engages us—things like beans, salt, and banks, to name three of the above. We won't remember thirty words; we will remember six, however, if they resonate emotionally—and surprises do just that.

The second reason for the emphasis on themes relates to memory. Slogans typically are designed to appear at the end of a commercial or the bottom of an advertisement, and we tend to best remember the last thing we see or hear.

And if marketers make those slogans surprising, of course, we remember them even better.

*   *   *

Why do we love rhymes, too?

In part, it's because rhymes work like riddles. Every first line makes us wonder, "How will it be answered?" The second line gives us closure, the closure that we have to hear, because our minds hate loose ends.

Rhymes also are play. That's all but proven by the name we give to exercises like rhyming: We call them word*play*. Play delights us, and what delights us sticks in our minds. That's why today, most of us read "I would not eat green eggs and ham. I do not like them" and immediately remember "Sam-I-am."

Which brings us to another collection of slogans from the Advertising Slogan Hall of Fame:

It takes a licking and keeps on ticking. (Timex)
Plop plop fizz fizz, oh what a relief it is. (Alka-Seltzer)
The quicker picker upper. (Bounty paper towels)
When you got it, flaunt it. (Braniff International Airways)
Please don't squeeze the Charmin. (Charmin toilet paper)

Great persuaders know that rhymes trick us; when words rhyme easily, we assume there is a genuine relationship between them. It's the force behind Jesse Jackson, a persuader so devoted to rhyme that Jay Leno once announced that Osama bin Laden tried to hire Jackson because "they are having trouble coming up with anything that rhymes with 'Taliban'."

So we are more prone to believe that haste must make waste, even though we've also been told the opposite in a less memorable nonrhyme: "He who hesitates is lost." The rhyme "Haste makes waste" sticks and sounds truer to us than the phrase that doesn't.

If you doubt this, you're not alone. The psychologist Matthew McGlorne of the University of Texas doubted it, too. So he ran a test. He showed subjects the expression "Woes unite foes" and a second expression with the identical idea: "Woes unite enemies."

What happened?

The subjects were far more apt to believe the rhyming version than the nonrhyming one. Rhymes just sound like they must be right, or as someone put it nicely, "There is reason in rhyme."

And was his understanding of this what led Johnnie Cochran to create for O. J. Simpson's jury the memorable rhyme/closing argument "If it doesn't fit, you must acquit"?

Whatever the explanation, rhythms and rhymes get us and trick us. They always have.

Issaquah's Wizards of Surprise

In 2008, Costco began offering on its website a unique canary diamond ring. The center stone weighed 10.61 carats, and the International Gemological Institute, which certifies diamond values, certified that it was worth $264,765.

A $5,000 diamond ring being offered for sale in a store known for enormous discounts surprises most people; a 10.61-carat ring that only Harry Winston might carry—and lend to Nicole Kidman on Oscar night—startles everyone.

Costco offered the ring for $180,000: $84,000 off! We had to notice.

Costco's canary diamond presents a surprise so big that it ventures into the realm of jokes. Costco's diamond is the equivalent of the lead item in the Neiman Marcus annual Christmas catalog, which each year features startling gifts such as his-and-her mummy cases and hot-air balloons.

Surprises like these draw crowds into Costco and make millions of people eagerly open Neiman's Christmas catalog. As the kids that we remain forever, we love surprises.

But these two surprises also are tricks. They set what decision-making experts and some readers know as anchors.

Our brains work around anchors. Studies show, for example, that if we flashed the number 1,120 at the beginning of this paragraph, then asked a paragraph later, "How many words are in the Gettysburg Address?" the average answer from readers would hover around 1,120. If we flashed the number 370 instead, however, the answer would hover around that number. (No one knows the correct answer—there are at least five known versions of the Gettysburg Address—but historians agree that 256 words is the best estimate.)

So we walk into a Costco and see a $180,000 ring. At this point, what is our idea of an expensive item? How cheap does a $145 espresso machine suddenly sound? After we see his-and-hers robots for $225,000 each, how can we not buy those little items priced only in four figures? (This also explains why Ralph Lauren offers an alligator bag for a mere $16,995. It makes us wonder how someone can possibly pass up the $1,695 leather bag.)

A few readers, reflecting on this example and the example of Costco exploiting our love of play, might find themselves thinking, "Yes, but I've never noticed a Costco ad or commercial."

No, you haven't. There aren't any.

Rather than try to leverage the force of conventional push marketing, Costco appeals to our love of surprise and play, and to great effect. Founded less than thirty years ago, the wizards of Issaquah have created America's third-largest retailer, its twenty-fourth-largest company, and one of the strongest cases anywhere for the power of appealing to our love of surprise and play.

III. OUR FIRST LOVE: STORIES

———

The Story Behind *60 Minutes*

On September 24, 1968, CBS Television introduced a new idea to Americans: a "television newsmagazine" named *60 Minutes.*

No black background and ticking stopwatch introduced the first show. Because documentaries on American television had missed more often than they'd hit, Alpo Dog Food was the only sponsor CBS could secure. The show opened with Harry Reasoner and Mike Wallace, and with stories about presidential candidates Hubert Humphrey and Richard Nixon, followed by several "articles" related to politics.

Patterned on a Canadian program, *60 Minutes*

looked like a gamble, and the overnight ratings showed it. The first show and those that followed rated only a little higher than the average documentary, but they weren't documentaries. They were articles in a television newsmagazine. That was unfamiliar.

The network tried to hold on, and the show slowly gained traction—very slowly. It took eight years to finally crack the Nielsen Top 20, but as more people watched, more people watched. Just three seasons later and eleven years after that opening program, *60 Minutes* reached number one for the first time.

Today, we know that CBS's gamble worked. *60 Minutes* is the longest continuously running prime-time television show in history. Its status as America's number-one program for five years is an achievement equaled only by *All in the Family* and *The Cosby Show*; and for every year from 1977 to 2000, it finished in the top ten in the Nielsen ratings, also a record.

60 Minutes obviously tapped something deep within us. What was it? Producer and mastermind Don Hewitt has said that the reason for the program's success is as old as the Bible.

The title of Hewitt's autobiography hints at this: It's called *Tell Me a Story*. Interviewed about the program for the PBS program *American Masters,* Hewitt explained: "Even the people who wrote the Bible were smart enough to know: Tell them a story. The issue was evil; the story was Noah. I latched on to that."

Hewitt had learned that storytelling is universal. Our ancestors covered their caves with the PowerPoint presentations of their time: the images they painted to tell stories about the hunt. Then and now, we need stories; a story is a single coherent whole that makes sense out of a lot of parts. Aesop, Jesus, Muhammad, Moses, Confucius, and followers of the Buddha all knew it; every religion has stories at its center.

For years before his death, journalists and journalism students would ask Hewitt the secret of his success, and his message was for everyone in any business. How do you get into our hearts and souls? Hewitt answered with a message today's best marketers heed: "At *60 Minutes*, we do what *everyone* should be doing: *Tell me a story.* Learn to do that, and you'll be a success."

The Great Communicator's Secret

Just before noon, eastern time, on January 28, 1986, on a subfreezing day on Merritt Island, Florida, the space shuttle *Challenger* exploded in a cloudless sky seventy-three seconds after takeoff. None of the seven crew members survived. That night, a visibly shaken President Ronald Reagan addressed the nation with a speech now considered among the greatest in American history. This is how he concluded:

> There's a coincidence today. On this day three hundred and ninety years ago, the great explorer Sir Francis Drake died aboard ship off the coast of Panama. In his lifetime the great frontiers were the oceans, and a historian later said, "He lived by the sea, died on it, and was buried in it." Well, today, we can say of the *Challenger* crew: Their dedication was, like Drake's, complete....We will never forget them, nor the last time we saw them, this morning, as they... waved goodbye and "slipped the surly bonds of earth" to "touch the face of God."

Known as the Great Communicator, Reagan did what great communicators do: He told stories. On August 28, 1963, at the Lincoln Memorial in Washington, D.C., Martin Luther King, Jr., did, too. King told stories of a dream, one that included sons of former slaves and slave owners "in the red hills of Georgia" sitting down together at tables, and those stories moved people and made them remember King's words decades later, when *American Rhetoric* named it the greatest speech in our history.

On his night, Reagan told two stories—one of Drake and the other of the *Challenger* crew repeating Drake's heroics—because he knew the power stories have over people. Undoubtedly, he learned that from his fifty-year film career in Hollywood. Actors act out stories, and we flock to see them.

How much do we crave stories? Consider Netflix, which CEO Reed Hastings started in 1997 after getting hit with a $40 late fee for *Apollo 13*. Every day, Hastings' company sends stories in the form of movies to subscribers nationwide. In just the fifty-five seconds that passed while you read this passage to this point, Netflix shipped eleven thousand of those stories.

Because of our passion for stories as well as play, is it any wonder the marketers at Pixar chose for the title of their blockbuster series of movies *Toy Story*?

We love stories. Perhaps best of all from every marketer's perspective, we remember them, as the next childhood story illustrates.

George Eliot's Grandfather's Wild Ride

One of many Americans' first lessons in the psychology of memory and the power of stories came in fourth grade. That's when we confronted the daunting task of learning to spell the word "geography."

Fortunately, many of our teachers gave us the mnemonic device that made spelling that long word easy. They gave us a story: George Eliot's old grandfather rode a pig home yesterday.

Why do we remember that sentence, with its nine words and forty-seven letters, more easily than we remember the nine letters in the word "geography"?

There are two reasons. George Eliot's old grandfather rode a pig home yesterday is a story, and we remember a single story better than we remember a sequence of letters, especially sequences longer than five letters. A famous piece of research, the Rule of Seven, Plus or Minus Two, holds that we can remember seven items, plus or minus two. (Perhaps the best example: You can remember phone numbers without area codes [seven digits] but not those with them [ten digits].) "Geography," having nine letters, is right on the limit of our capacity to remember, according to this theory.

Second, while stories are more memorable than simple narrative sentences—which explains why we are able to remember entire jokes, because they are a single story—certain stories are more easily remembered. As we learn from jokes, we are more apt to remember a surprising story.

The pig-riding story surprises us. The image of an old man steering a pig, especially all the way home, amuses us. And it puzzles us, too. How can an old man ride a pig? Pigs hug the ground so closely; where does he put his feet to get them out of ground's way? And pigs move very slowly. So why would he ever choose one to ride sixty feet, much less "all the way home"?

We remember George Eliot's story because it doesn't give us nine things to remember, like the word "geography." It gives us just five:

The boy's name: George Eliot
His relative: old grandfather
His mode of transport: a pig
Where he went: home
When: yesterday

This gives us what memory experts call chunks, and we remember in chunks. The George Eliot story has just five chunks, as opposed to the nine chunks in the word "geography." But then comes the final step, the one that explains why storytelling is used in all cultures in all times. As with all stories, after we repeat a story several times, it turns into a single chunk—and nothing is easier to remember than a single chunk.

J. Peterman's Fantasies

Time was we bought shirts, ties, blouses, jeans. It was simple.

Then the stuff piled up, and we had trouble telling it all apart. Jeans were jeans were jeans. And then they weren't.

Among the people who changed this was a Kentuckian with a catalog. He dreamed of owning a Duesenberg, it seems. Or so one of his tiny odes in his famous catalog suggests.

He was, and is, J. Peterman. His distinctive catalog of things—a Marie Antoinette nightshirt and a Gatsby shirt—might have earned him a few million dollars. But his style of storytelling transformed him from a success in business into a frequent character on *Seinfeld*.

Peterman's notoriety rested on sentences that rarely exceeded twelve words. Sometimes he used five words. Other times, three. His simplicity drew people in. Simplicity always does.

But the real seduction in Peterman's words came from how he assembled them: He made them into stories. So a Peterman shirt was never just a shirt; it was Jay Gatsby's shirt, just as a black dress was Audrey Hepburn's, with the only extra being a string of pearls. (Aware of the appeal of detail, from Peterman's keyboard this would have come out "a string of pearls, from a favorite shop just off the Rue du Montaigne.")

Peterman knew that like child, like adult: We are captivated by stories, eager from their suspense to know what comes next. So thousands of us, including Oprah Winfrey and Frank Sinatra, bought Peterman's stories, and then his items.

A typical Peterman entry:

Versailles Hoof-Pick Belt (No. 2580). Made in the heart of Kentucky horse country by Claire Painter.
Who's she?
A gifted artisan, right in my backyard.
Claire worked as a master saddle maker in Perthshire, Scotland. Then, thankfully, she moved here.
The leather is from Wicket and Craig, which has been producing the finest leather goods in North America for the past century and a half.
The buckle, solid brass, is an actual working hoof pick, not a replica.
One of the finest pieces I've ever seen.

There's just one problem: People will never stop asking you about it.

Can you live with that?

Peterman doesn't sell just a belt; he sells the story behind it, which gives the belt meaning. It's no longer a belt with a solid brass buckle, but the creation of a former master saddle maker from Scotland who somehow ended up in Lexington, Kentucky. Plus that brass buckle isn't a buckle at all; it's a working hoof pick, which sounds like a one-of-a-kind touch, not to mention something we might use one day to pick a horse hoof.

Peterman's fame reminds us how much we love stories.

But wait, you say. Didn't Peterman's company end up struggling? It has. It once declared bankruptcy. Does this mean we are less susceptible to stories than it appears?

No. Peterman's problem stemmed from what followed.

We ordered one of his remarkable items—a black dress that Audrey Hepburn might have worn, say. Days later, our coveted box arrived from Kentucky. We breathlessly opened the parcel.

But what?

Our Hepburn dress arrived encased in cheap clear plastic wrap and had taken a pounding in transit, producing wrinkles that Audrey never would have tolerated. Nothing in the package reminds us of Audrey or her story. Seeing her dress sprawling on the bed, we see just a wrinkled cotton dress—not Egyptian cotton, or cotton from Sea Island, but perhaps a decent strain grown in Kentucky—with no obvious detail that helps us understand why an iconic actress ever would have chosen that dress.

The story was over, the romance was gone.

The problem with J. Peterman stories was that they were fictional, and we buy the real stories behind products—or at least, what we believe are the real stories. When we learn that Häagen-Dazs isn't from Scandinavia but from the Bronx, for example, and that the founder made up the name because it sounded Scandinavian to him, that story devolves into mere fantasy and we lose interest—and perhaps some faith.

J. Peterman created interesting stories, but we don't buy interesting stories; we buy the interesting true stories that today's best marketers tell.

The Storytellers of Stumptown

In its March 9, 2010, issue, *Time* magazine announced that Starbucks might have met its David.

A rival coffee from nearby Portland, Oregon, had emerged. America's foremost coffee expert, Oliver Strand of the *New York Times*, went a step further in the article: "Stumptown is the new leader."

To Stumptown's charismatic founder, Duane Sorenson, coffee is like wine, with an elevation, a quality of land (the *terroir*), a varietal, and tasting notes printed on every bag. (We learn that Sumatra Lake Tawar's notes, for example, are blackberry cobbler, star anise, and cannabis.)

Here is Stumptown's website description of one of its nineteen varietals:

> Geisha is an extremely rare coffee varietal that has made waves in the past 5+ years for having what many coffee connoisseurs consider to be the most brilliantly complex and intense flavor profile of all. Originally brought to Costa Rica from the small town of Gesha in southwestern Ethiopia, the geisha made its way south to Panama, thanks to Don Pachi (Francisco Serracin), before becoming internationally acclaimed. These trees grow to be very tall and have beautiful, elongated leaves....

Sorenson is drawing us into the deeper meaning of each Stumptown cup. In Geisha's case, she's a little bean from a small town that found her way to a bigger city thanks to a man named Francisco, and then to international acclaim: She's the little bean that could.

Eventually, this draws us into Sorenson's story. The bearded son of a sausage maker from Puyallup, Washington, he dropped out of Seattle University, wears hoodies and black Adidas high-tops, adores AC/DC, and lives in an apartment crammed with a dozen French presses. He's a little guy, too, on a mission: He Jeeps his way into outbacks all over the world to find world's great varietals.

The nearby Abercrombie & Fitch stores are built around stories, too. We hear it from CEO Michael Jeffries, who compares his stores to movies: "I want people walking in and wondering, "What's at the box office today?" His clothing reveals this, too, portraying itself as the well-worn sweatshirts from a New York State championship winning team and from a summer camp at "Camp Beaver Tail," membership in "The Growlers," and nights spent with buddies at "Warrior's Tap."

Without some story to give it meaning, products are just stuff. Sorenson and Jeffries and the astute modern merchandisers realize this and turn to something universal that we love: a story.

The Moral of Two Stories: Nike and Scion

One overcast Monday morning in February 1973, two third-year students at the University of Oregon School of Law approached a second-year student with a memorable request. Two fellow Oregonians had started a company and were raising additional capital. The two students insisted the company would succeed. How would you like to invest $2,000? They were sure that student—me—could triple my money.

Oh sure, I thought, running shoes will be big.

Their optimistic prediction turned out to be off by millions. Their friend was Phil Knight, the company was Nike, and Nike's success is often viewed as a testament to brilliant marketing and lucky timing.

There was much more to it. We can dispose of luck, which always matters, and of which Nike had plenty. The first came from a disaster: the 1972 Munich Olympics. Everything about that Olympics foretold doom for Americans: suspicious disqualifications of American gold-medal hopefuls in swimming and the pole vault and unexpected failures by Americans in other events.

All of this became trivial when at 4:30 a.m. on

Sunday, September 5, Palestinian terrorists broke into the Olympic Village and forced their way into the rooms of members of the Israeli Olympics team. During that entry, they killed two of the members, then took nine more hostage, eventually to a Boeing 727 waiting at a nearby airport.

Less than twenty-four hours after those terrorists entered the athletes' rooms came an unforgettable announcement from sleepless and teary NBC sportscaster Jim McKay, for years the voice of the Games: "They're all gone."

Against this hideous background, and after days during which the games were suspended, the marathon was run. For the Americans watching, the prevailing feeling was "What possibly could happen next?"

And what happened next changed the face of America for decades.

A gaunt and relatively unknown Yale Law School student named Frank Shorter took the early lead, and for miles ran alone toward the finish. Fearing the worst in this worst of all Olympics, America watched, but the worst never came. What came instead was Shorter's win. That night, Americans watched the highlights of the race set to McKay's riveting prose, including his unforgettable words about the marathon itself, repeated like the hook of a song: "You must run the race by yourself."

What happened the next day in America was reminiscent of February 10, 1964, the Monday after American teenage boys first saw the Beatles and showed up at school with their short hair combed forward, Beatle-like. After Shorter's win, Americans copied him. They started jogging, then running. But they quickly learned that their old white Converse low-cut basketball shoes or Keds didn't work. They needed running shoes instead. And Phil Knight noticed.

Knight was a former above-average miler at the University of Oregon, a school in a town, Eugene, that is hallowed among distance runners. It suggests that small town's stature in the world of running that it once held not just one marathon but two—one marathon for every 42,000 residents. The first was called the Nike OTC (Oregon Track Club) Marathon, and it attracted most of America's best marathoners. The second was called the Track Capital Marathon, a title the town had held for years.

Beginning in the mid-1950s and continuing for decades after, many of America's best young distance runners chose the University of Oregon for the opportunity to train under the school's famous coach, Bill Bowerman.

In the fall of 1970, Bowerman attracted one more person who would figure prominently in Nike's story. He was a 5-foot-9-inch, 145-pound package of sheer will from the small Oregon coastal town of Coos Bay. He was Steve Prefontaine, and he became iconic, too, breaking eight NCAA records and winning seven NCAA titles in his career. Today, you see people in "Pre Lives" T-shirts from Tampa to Kuala Lumpur, and every serious runner knows what those words mean.

Through his decades of work with runners including Pre, Bowerman had become dissatisfied with the Adidas and Tiger shoes made for distance runners. Those shoes tended to be barely modified versions of the shoes worn by sprinters, who run almost exclusively on their forefeet and do not need arch support or heel cushioning. But distance runners train and race on paved roads and concrete. They don't need speed or spikes; they need cushioning from the pounding.

Famously puzzling over this problem in his kitchen one morning, Bowerman took a waffle iron, injected it with a rubberized compound, and made a sole for a running shoe. The sole naturally looked like an inverted waffle; square studs protruded from where the waffle holes normally would be. The waffle sole was a welcome and needed innovation, and runners quickly embraced it.

So Nike's story now included Eugene, the nation's track capital; the University of Oregon, distance running's Mecca; Bowerman, running's distinguished elder statesman; Pre, America's premier distance runner and most charismatic figure; and the most innovative shoe in the sport.

This was the Nike story, and its truth resonated in a way no other athletic shoe company's story could.

By contrast, what was the Adidas story?

Adidas's story was created by a German unknown to Americans. He was and still is so unknown that few Americans know that the name "Adidas" comes from the name of the company's founder, Adi Dasler.

And what was the Puma story?

A family feud: Adi and his Adidas partner and brother started fighting one day. In a huff, the brother left Adidas and started Puma as an act of revenge against Adi.

Adidas and Puma are German companies, which gives them weak running backstories. When Nike emerged, world and European distance running had been dominated by the Kenyans, the Finnish, and some Eastern Europeans—but not the Germans. The only German runner of brief note was Waldemar Cierpinski, but he hailed from East Germany and was tainted by stories of the East German athletic machine and its use of steroids. So the German running story, such as it was, had few chapters.

What was Tiger's story?

Tiger was based in Japan, a country without a significant distance-running tradition other than its well-known marathon in Fukuoka, which owed what little fame it had in America to the fact that Shorter won it the year before his Olympic win and in each of the three years after.

Nike won its race, in part, because no competitors could match its story. Nike was more than a manufacturer; it was a collection of running purists who wanted to help people run and train for long distances in something more than a thin, flat sole glued to a synthetic upper and tied together with string.

Nike's founders realized the power of its story and the influence it would have. Its first ads didn't even feature its shoes but told the stories of the renegades behind them. An early single-page ad focused on Bowerman himself, under the headline "The Spirit That Moves Us." Nike's very noncorporate-looking "top executives" were featured in another early ad. They were shown sitting in an airport gate waiting area, clad in clothes several degrees short of business casual, with the headline: "Our first employees are still with us. We think." Nike told us they were traveling the world, trying to help runners run better.

Nike told its story well, in a voice more like a conversation than a corporate ad, trumpeting the standard "We listen, we're with you all the way." Runners knew Nike cared about them, for an obvious and compelling reason: Nike was them, and runners wanted to be a part of them.

When Nike expanded into other sports, it routinely brought on the best athletes in those sports—Michael Jordan and Tiger Woods most vividly—not just for the endorsement value but the meaning behind it: We are the shoes for the truly serious athletes, the shoes that help you Just Do It—whatever your "It" is.

We don't buy things; we buy what they mean, and a company's stories provide that meaning. We need narratives from birth to comprehend our world and everything in it.

Nike knew that, because Nike knew—intensely—precisely what runners love. But of course they did; they were the very runners they were trying to appeal to. Nike wasn't tapping a market; it *was* the market.

Compare Nike's success selling to runners to Toyota's efforts to capture the attention of America's youth and sell its entry-level Scion by identifying itself with hip-hop. Hip-hop's signal characteristics are graffiti, break dancing, MC'ing and Dj'ing, rebellion, and slang; Toyota's are making and selling well-made, low-defect, affordable cars. Nike's connection to runners was and is real and undeniable; Toyota's hip-hop connection, like its cars, has been totally manufactured.

This may help explain the Scion's twin fates: Scions prospered at first, but largely because the wrong people kept buying them: older drivers looking for affordable vehicles that were easy to get into and out of, and parents who finally found an inexpensive car with lots of space for maneuvering children into and out of car seats. Perhaps because too many hip-hoppers noticed all these retirees and parents behind "their" wheels, Scion sales started dropping drastically in 2009.

Nike didn't try to target the running culture; it *was* the running culture. It didn't have to concoct stories about its role in running; they were everywhere you looked. Scion, by contrast, took the conventional aim strategy: Let's target a segment and ingratiate ourselves with the people in it, even to the point of making it appear that Scion is not really a Toyota. On its website, the only references to Toyota are those required by law, and they appear in the smallest typeface allowed by law.

The Scion lacks a story; no story links it to hip-hop. And today, it's stories—authentic stories, told well—that win, just as stories have captured us from those nights with Mom and Dad reading at our bedsides.

IV. LITTLE VERSUS BIG

———

The Moral of a Hundred Childhood Stories

In our childhoods, we heard about David slaying Goliath and about the bad giant who fee-fi-foe-fummed about the blood of an Englishman. Had we grown up in New Delhi or Oslo, one hundred years ago or even a thousand, we would have heard similar giant stories; they are universal.

The giants in these myths are the same: They are scary and—fortunately for the hero—stupid. Giants also are unholy; they war with the gods. In different story versions, Goliath was a pagan, a representative of Satan, or both.

From childhood, we equate big with evil.

We do it instantly with the wolf. He is not just big but bad: the big bad wolf. Oafs are not small, either;

they are big oafs. Slovenly people are never small but always fat and big: they are big fat slobs.

Godzilla, the T. rex, the great white whale of *Moby Dick*, the great white shark of *Jaws*: the huge offends and terrifies us.

Hearing these stories, we identify with the small characters: Little Bo Peep, Little Jack Horner, Little Boy Blue, or Little Miss Muffet, one of the girls from *Little Women* or the boy in *The Little Prince*. Later, we root for *Little Orphan Annie* and the *Little Mermaid,* and later still for *Little Miss Sunshine.* We adopt as our symbol of American persistence a small locomotive: *The Little Engine That Could.*

In George Orwell's harrowing view in *1984*, Big Brother controls us. Politicians promise us that they "look out for the little guy," arouse us by deploring Big Government, and often help wage the battle against Big Oil.

Big businesses suffer bad press. They are staffed with *The Man in the Gray Flannel Suit*, the cube dwellers, the clueless bosses in *Dilbert*. We view Big Business as business but equate small business with art; we call it entrepreneurship. The suffix of that word, *-ship*, connotes goodness and skill, as we see in the words "sportsmanship," "craftsmanship," "leadership," and "scholarship."

The word "entrepreneur" also sounds artistic, and it should. The word comes from the French, who first used the word to denote a leader in the arts: specifically, the director of a musical institution.

The leader of a business engages in the act of being busy—literally, *busy ness*—and makes things. An entrepreneur, by contrast, engages in artistry; she makes music or something closely akin to it.

It goes further. We call large companies businesses but refer to small ones as enterprises, and to be enterprising, as the *Random House Dictionary* reminds us, is to be "characterized by a bold daring energetic spirit." Businesses are characterized by profit and loss, but enterprises are bold and daring; they are the starship *Enterprise*s of our day, boldly going "where no man has gone before."

We revere the Thomas Edisons who started these great enterprises, even though many, including Edison, proved totally incapable of running them. We regularly nod at the old saw "Behind every great fortune is a great crime." That's what our ancestors said of the men who founded America's first huge industries, oil and the railroads; they dubbed them Robber Barons. In that tradition, a generation of American journalists called the muckrakers became famous by exposing the alleged misdeeds of Standard Oil and other large businesses.

In 1973, a British economist named E. F. Schumacher printed a series of essays in a book whose title became part of our American business vernacular: *Small Is Beautiful.* The title derives from Schumacher's quotation, straight from the pages of David and Goliath: "Man is small. Therefore, small is beautiful."

In 1995, Alan Webber and Bill Taylor followed Schumacher's lead and launched the magazine *Fast Company,* focusing on the smaller technology companies they saw transforming our culture. Their choice of title reflects a popular view: Small companies are fast, not the plodding Goliaths that dominate the pages of *Forbes* and *Fortune.*

Fortune noticed *Fast Company*'s success and began morphing into a magazine that now insists on staying current on Twitter, Facebook, and Skype, and that each year devotes relatively more columns to the Davids than the Goliaths on which it once focused totally. On its website, *Fortune* constantly updates a section devoted to computing's David, Apple.

The David language also reflects a popular American view of Big Business: Giants are evil. Apple's employees and fans calls their enemy, Microsoft, the Evil Empire, a title that tech hackers once attached to IBM. Five minutes away in Mountain View, Sergey Brin and Larry Page rally their masses at Google behind a telling battle cry: Don't be evil.

Watch where we congregate in cities on

weekends: Greenwich Village in New York, Ybor City in Tampa, Twenty-Third Street in Portland, Gaslamp Quarter in San Diego, and Capitol Hill in Seattle. They are skyscraper-free. The Yuma Building looms as a towering monument in Gaslamp at just three stories. Many of the restaurants on Twenty-Third Street are in old homes. Others flee even those small places to small towns like Chatham, Cannon Beach, and Carmel, where a three-story building would look alien.

Given our choice, we flee big and head to small. We've been doing it almost from the moment our cities' buildings started scraping their skies. Headlines bemoan the flight from our inner cities, but do the editors realize what we are doing? We are acting out Little vs. Big.

You can see it in our choice of these urban areas and weekend favorites and in our choice of words. How do we describe an inviting, small restaurant? We call it "intimate," which suggests that small is personal and big is not; and we call it "cozy," a reminder that small makes us comfortable and big makes us uneasy.

It's this realization that drove the creation of Disneyland and Disney World. A visitor there easily misses the trick its designers have played. The buildings aren't normal. They are two-thirds scale by design; the wizards of Disney knew about Little vs. Big, as you might expect of a company that is built around children and the stories from our childhood, like *Swiss Family Robinson* and *Sleeping Beauty*. The parks are big yet feel little and accessible, and we feel bigger when we walk their paths.

Look at the ascendancy of the dollar stores. Their prices are appealing, but their scale is made to be, too: a Family Dollar and Dollar General Store takes up just 6,500 square feet, while a Dollar Tree isn't much bigger than many homes, at just 3,900 square feet. Abercrombie & Fitch stores work Little vs. Big, too, squeezing into intimate spaces and highlighting them with dark, intimate lighting, leather couches, rugs, and foliage, a feeling accentuated by the low ceilings. Welcome to our little home.

Which bring us to the trials of Ford and General Motors. Do they struggle not just because healthcare costs add almost $2,000 to the cost of each American car, or because other American labor costs are high, or because GM created too many brands that no one could tell apart? Or do they struggle because they succeeded?

Did Ford and GM succeed and from that grow too big for us? They became giants, and we do not believe in "Too big to fail." We believe that becoming big dooms one to failure.

So our government had to rescue Ford and GM because few of us would. We don't trust giants; we never have.

On the night of April 8, 2009, a short, stout, and unemployed lady appears on the stage of *Britain's Got Talent,* the U.K.'s version of our *American Idol.* She tells the judges she is forty-seven and has never been kissed; we believe her, as the wicked big judge Simon Cowell rolls his eyes. Just as she is about to sing, the camera focuses on the handsome judge with the kinder face. Even that nice fellow is chuckling.

A pause.

Susan Boyle sings the first line, and when she hits the fifth note, the camera pans across the three judges' faces; their eyes are open wide. The crowd is clapping, soon to be shouting. At twenty seconds, they are standing and shouting. The pretty judge Amanda raises her hands to her face, and we sense her tears coming. And ours, too.

It is the great American story enacted on a British stage, and it reaches America in minutes. Watching on YouTube, covered with goose bumps, we watch that mean Simon Cowell beam, and others watch by the multimillions. Over the next thirty days, a single clip of Boyle's performance attracts 78 million hits on YouTube—exactly one hit every second.

Americans are famous for our love of under-dogs like Susan Boyle. Underdogs demonstrate a truth we hold self-evident: that because we all are created equal, we all are capable of extraordinary things—becoming president, starting a billion-dollar company, writing the Great American Novel from a house in foreclosure. Underdogs confirm our very American faith in the Little Man, the Little Prince, the Little Engine That Could.

So when Susan Boyle serenaded the world, the people in our country cheered the loudest. We cried, too, not least of all because she and the producers chose the perfect American underdog song for her, as clever a piece of scripting as you will ever see: They had her sing "I Dreamed a Dream."

Apple understands Susan Boyle's appeal to us. In Apple's Mac vs. PC commercials, the Mac char-acter is played by actor Justin Long. A stray brown hair over 5 feet 8 inches and a Red Bull over 145 pounds, Long looks like a chill kid who in high school might have been named "Most Likely Not to Appear in Class," which he was.

The PC character is played by actor John Hodg-man. Seven years older and many pounds heavier than Long, Hodgman looks like a guy who played viola in his high school orchestra, which he did.

Apple's ads work Little vs. Big, the likable little underdog, as Apple always has. Justin Longish and defying upperdog convention, skinny Steve Jobs makes all his major appearances wearing nondesigner jeans and white New Balance running shoes. Microsoft's John Hodgmanish CEO Steve Ballmer makes his major appearances in button-down shirts, slacks, and polished leather shoes. The mostly young tech-business press covers Ballmer, whom *Business Week* once described as being "built like a linebacker," respectfully; they treat skinny Steve Jobs with wonder. Jobs knows they love an underdog, and like Ben & Jerry and the folks at Mini Cooper, he and his company constantly play that role and earn our special affection.

Underdogs in the Mist

You walk into Irvine Spectrum mall in Irvine, California, and quickly notice an odd store. What gets your attention is the name: There isn't one. Instead, the store sports three logos on the front: 6.0, Hurley, and Converse.

You walk into No Name, notice the snowboarding and skateboarding merchandise, and eventually ask, "Who is behind this?"

The answer is Nike. Nike makes 6.0 products and acquired Hurley in 2002 and Converse a year later. Then why isn't the Nike name on the store?

The answer is Goliath. Nike knows that younger customers, particularly skateboarders and snowboarders, see themselves as renegades and underdogs and are at that age where big looks particularly odious. To them, as Nike's Jeanne Jackson reaffirms, "It's not cool to have a big hairy name over the door."

David and Goliath thinking also prompted the creation in late 2008 of a new bus service aimed at the urban young and newly shrewd: BoltBus. By offering leather seats, ample leg room, and the perk of the decade, free WiFi, Bolt boldly distances itself from that old bus line that even sounds like our granddad, Greyhound. There's just one catch: With the deft help of the Sausalito, California, ad agency Butler, Shine, Stern & Partners, it was Greyhound that created, and now owns, BoltBus.

It's a misty March afternoon in Seattle, and you've made your way to the center of the city's counterculture, the Capitol Hill neighborhood.

The Hill offers a remarkable mix. It's the neighborhood that gave the world grunge and Seattle's first millionaires the perfect site for their homes. You come onto the 600 block of Fourteenth Avenue and see one right after another the three-story brick and Tudor mansions of Seattle's Millionaires' Row.

Once off Fourteenth, everywhere else you look is a coffeehouse: Caffe Ladro, Caffé Vita, Café Dharwin, Fuel Coffee, Insomniax, Stumptown, People's Republic of Koffee, B&O Espresso (where Pearl Jam came up with its name), Online Coffee. You notice one Victrola Coffee and Art, then a second, and on Broadway, a Starbucks, but of course, this is Starbucks' hometown.

On Fifteenth Avenue you notice a particularly intriguing looking spot: 15th Ave Coffee and Tea. Inside, your eyes go immediately to its massive stainless steel espresso machine. You strain to read the barely legible logo on its burnished surface. It reads La Marzocco. You imagine that 15th Ave's owner spotted this machine in a Rome coffeehouse and bought it from the Italian owner who was about to retire.

You are close. The owners purchased the machine new from Florence, Italy, where La Marzocco has made these machines since 1929, famous for brewing every cup within a half-degree Celsius of every other.

The owners seem to have worked the nearby antique stores: a set of 1930s-era wooden theater seats flank the aged blonde oak chairs around the tables. It's the hip classic coffeehouse you might find if the hipster owners had huge trust funds.

You're impressed. You decide this place might give Starbucks a run.

But this store isn't a threat to Starbucks, even at a time when Starbucks has closed 961 stores in one year and laid off 6,700 employees over two years; it's Starbucks' counterattack. Howard Schultz and his team decided it needed to innovate, and this test shop was one response. There's a subtle clue of this on the 15th Ave sign. It reads "Inspired by Starbucks."

There's no question what you are seeing: a Little strategy. 15th Ave makes that explicit in its promotions, saying it promotes small local music groups to perform in the evenings and uses products from selected small farmers. (The Caribou Coffee chain executes its Little strategy with similar words, promising that its teas and oatmeals are "handcrafted," for example.)

This strategy is Starbucks' approach to what many call "The Big Coffee problem" and for which the owner of the rival Victrola Coffee chose the perfect words to conclude this section: "The Goliath is coming at me under a new name."

THE FORCES AND
THEIR SOURCES

2. OUR CULTURE

I. Me: The Great
Individualists

As the primary drafter of our Declaration of Independence, thirty-three-year-old Thomas Jefferson could have set as America's goal "liberty, equality, and fraternity," the words the French chose for their declaration thirteen years later, but he chose "life, liberty, and the pursuit of happiness" instead. The French seemed to declare, "We're all in this together"; Jefferson seemed to declare, "We're all in this for ourselves."

Have Jefferson's famous seven words told generations of us to look out for ourselves?

It certainly seems that way in 2011. Scan a bookshelf today, and you will see that our pursuit of happiness has become a daylong sprint. In 2000, publishers issued forty books on the subject. Eight years later, they released an average of fifteen new books on happiness *every day*.

What Howard Hughes and 50 Cent Showed Us

Curtis James Jackson III began pursuing wealth when he was twelve years old by selling cocaine in his home neighborhood of Queens, New York. He's succeeded. One of his homes recently was valued at $24 million, thanks in major part to the popularity of his CD *Get Rich or Die Tryin'*. Now famous under the name 50 Cent, Curtis might seem the embodiment of American materialism and the perfect person to answer the question "What is the meaning of money?"

We might expect him to answer, "Bling, Benzes, and booty." But we hear from him something truly American instead. "Money," he says, "is freedom."

True materialists crave things. Americans don't; we merely stockpile them. The Midwest auto dealer Denny Hecker declared bankruptcy and was found to own nine Rolex watches. If Hecker valued a Rolex watch, he would own one, but he doesn't. He owns nine. It's not his Rolexes; they satisfy no Hecker urge.

Buying things is only sometimes about owning the things. Buying often is simply about what 50 Cent observed: being *able* to buy. Having less means hearing, "No, you cannot have that," and we loathe being told what we can and cannot do.

Being able to buy is an expression of our deepest value, the one we would die for: our freedom.

There's a perfect subject for testing this hypothesis, the icon who once personified the accumulation of wealth in America: Howard Hughes. Hughes tried to acquire everything; he even acquired a barber.

For seventeen years, Hughes paid Eddie Alexander generously—$7,000 in today's dollars for a single hair cut—to do nothing except be on permanent call for Hughes, day and night. At 2 a.m. one night, Hughes decided to test Alexander's devotion. He dialed his number and heard only one ring.

"That you, Howard?" Eddie answered, his clipper and shears nearby him.

"Just checking, Eddie, just checking."

The best words anyone could write about Hughes's apparent materialism have been written, crafted by Joan Didion in *Slouching Towards Bethlehem,* in an entry titled "7700 Romaine":

That we have made a hero of Howard Hughes tells us something interesting about ourselves...that the secret point of money and power in America is neither the things that money can buy nor power for power's sake...*but absolute personal freedom, mobility, privacy.* It is the instinct which drove America to the Pacific, all through the nineteenth century, the desire to be able to find a restaurant open in case you want a sandwich, to be a free agent, *live by one's own rules.*

Our ancestors' passions to be utterly free brought them here, and our Statue of Liberty beckoned to them, the masses "yearning to breathe free." Patrick Henry repeated the passion in famous form, "Give me liberty or give me death," and in 1971, the state of New Hampshire took up this cause and inscribed on every state license plate four famous words: Live Free or Die.

Like 50 Cent and Hughes and Henry, we crave the idea of freedom. Harley-Davidson knows this; its core message forever has been freedom: It's the American motorcycle that lets you feel free. Motorcyclists themselves vividly illustrate this when they rebel against helmet laws. We should be able to kill ourselves, they argue, a risk worth bearing so that we can feel the rush of air on our faces as we ride.

Our seemingly ludicrous proliferation of

choices—eighty-five kinds of snack crackers and entire racks full only of toothpaste—is our marketers' answer to the plea that we have freedom of choice. The more choices we have, the more American we feel.

In comparative political science, we learn about deferential cultures. Citizens in these cultures are inclined to follow rules and obey authority. Ours isn't one of them; we loathe being told what to do, and we are quick to justify our actions with a favorite American expression: "Hey, it's a free country."

This makes a particular form of behavior, which you can find in all cultures, particularly common in ours. Psychologists call it reactance, one of our cognitive biases that leads us to make bad decisions. It's our tendency to resist not just orders but also suggestions, because we dislike giving up our freedom.

Reactance explains why Valentine's retailers get disappointing results when they post banners like "Don't forget her flowers for Valentine's Day." Millions of men who see that message react by going to buy candy instead—unless the local candy retailer has a similar banner, "Don't forget her candy this Valentine's Day." In that case, they just take her out for an expensive dinner.

Can you find more reactant people than Americans? Rather than obey laws, we for decades have celebrated the men and women who break them. We cheered John Dillinger and Bonnie and Clyde, celebrating them in movies and literature. We love a good criminal.

(To those who suggest Americans liked those three people because they robbed banks, and bankers were often the scapegoats for the Great Depression, it's worth noting that Americans also celebrated Billy the Kid, Butch Cassidy, and the Sundance Kid—and those three men robbed anything that jingled.)

Americans love what producers call heist movies—*Reservoir Dogs, Heat, Mission: Impossible, The Heist, The Italian Job,* and, as perhaps the most vivid reminder, the parade of *Ocean's* films of the past decade: *Ocean's 11, 12,* and now *13.* ABC television, for years the most conservative purveyor of television shows, created a hit in 1968 by portraying Robert Wagner as a lovable thief, burglar, and pickpocket in the show *It Takes a Thief,* inspired by the 1955 hit Cary Grant movie *To Catch a Thief.*

In 2002, Steven Spielberg's casting left little doubt for whom we should root in *Catch Me If You Can.* So we cheered the handsome Leonardo DiCaprio playing the gifted con man Frank Abagnale as he eluded the cop played by the dogged and doughty Tom Hanks.

Everyone reading this must admit: We root for

the thieves, not the cops. The mafia titans portrayed in the *Godfather* series acted murderously, but as Don Corleone said, "It's just business." American audiences laughed at Corleone's remark, then booed the two biggest villains of the saga: the brutal Irish cop whom Al Pacino dispatches in *The Godfather* and the oily U.S. senator in *The Godfather: Part II.* In each case, we rooted for the crooks and against a character who enforced the laws and another character who made them.

We're outlaws at heart, are we not?

Getting Bonnies and Clydes to Buckle Up

For years, state governments, legitimately concerned about the losses of life attributable to drivers not wearing seat belts, waged earnest campaigns to get people to change. Nothing seemed to work. An extreme example of Americans' apparent indifference was a test performed on moviegoers.

Researchers put cameras in the parking lot of a theater to record how many people attending the movie had their seat belts fastened when they arrived. Once inside, the audience members were shown a film that graphically portrayed what had happened to several auto-crash victims who had not fastened their seat belts.

When the audience members left the theater and entered their cars, the same cameras ran. Like everyone reading this, the researchers assumed that many people who had arrived with their seat belts detached would attach them when they left, having seen the gory consequences of not buckling up.

But they didn't.

Not only did the nonbucklers stick to their apparent death wishes, but several bucklers did, too; *several who arrived wearing their seat belts left without buckling up.* "Try to trick me into fastening my belt—the hell with them!" they appeared to say with their acts of defiance.

These failed efforts led several state departments of public safety to try a new strategy. Instead of using the threat of death, they would remind drivers that the law requires them to wear their seat belts. Thus was born a series of campaigns with the simple theme "Buckle Up. It's the Law."

This didn't work, either. We want to be free.

What to do to get us to buckle up? Because we all pay dearly for traffic fatalities just in our added insurance premiums, the states could not afford to give up, and from their persistence emerged what seems an identical campaign, which the state of North Carolina initiated in 1993.

Their new message was "Click it or ticket," and at long last, it worked. Ten years later, the National Highway Traffic Safety Administration, which adopted the North Carolina plan, reported a greater than 10 percent increase in seat belt use by adults ages eighteen to twenty-four.

Why did that work when everything else failed?

Some of that increase can be traced to the memorableness of the theme itself. The two words "click it" give the theme three of the elements of memorable messages: brevity, rhyme, and surprise; few of us had heard the expression "click it" before.

But North Carolina's history-making message also delivers another implicit message that resonates in a nation of outlaws. It gives us a choice. We can buckle up or not. If we don't, we get a ticket. Our choice.

It's a free country. The message worked spectacularly where so many other messages failed. The others told us what do or tried to make us afraid. The state of North Carolina, however, gave us what we love most: freedom, in this case the freedom of choice.

And like Patrick Henry and 50 Cent, we responded.

The Solved Mystery of the $70 Watch

We are so obsessed with fairness that we will sacrifice for it in at least one unusual way.

It requires little effort to go online today and download free music. Sources such as Gnutella and Kazaa flourish, safe havens for music pirates. None of us needs to pay for music today.

But we do. Despite the music industry's desire to shut down these services that would seem to threaten the industry's survival, no one in that industry has proved that these pirate sites have resulted in fewer CDs being sold, and there is some evidence that these pirate sites have boosted interest in music and performers by letting fans sample the work. We keep paying for music.

There's probably something else at work here. We willingly pay 99 cents for "Sex on Fire," for example, because that price seems fair at least, perhaps even a steal, and because to pay Kings of Leon nothing might feel to us, quite reasonably, like theft. We are obsessed with fairness—for everyone. For years, we heard "Do unto others." In the case of music, at least, we willingly do just that.

This brings us nicely to a puzzle that for years has puzzled some scholars.

Here it is. You go to Target to buy a Casio watch and find one you want. It's listed at $70. Just as you pull out your credit card, a friend spots you and taps your shoulder. "They have that exact watch—the exact same—just three blocks away. And it's $40!"

Do you walk the three blocks to save the $30 on the Casio?

Now, part two: You go to Target to buy a Samsung DVD player, receiver, and set of speakers. It's $800. Just as you pull out your credit card, a friend notices you and taps your shoulder. "They have that same system—the exact same—just three blocks away. And it's $770!"

Do you walk the three blocks to save the $30—the same amount you'd save by walking three blocks for the watch?

To many people, these two questions seem similar, so our answer should be, too. If we'd walk three blocks to save $30, we should do it, whether it's for a $40 watch or a $770 stereo. And perhaps we would.

But millions of our fellow Americans wouldn't.

In these tests, great numbers of people who say they'd walk three blocks for the cheaper watch say they wouldn't walk three blocks for the cheaper stereo.

To many people, this behavior sounds inconsistent and foolish. To many students of American behavior, it seems utterly American.

Consider our origins. When the Pilgrims alit on Plymouth Rock, they were fleeing a country where they felt unfree, particularly to practice the religion of their choice. England was, then and now, a class system. If you were born right, life was good; if not, life seemed unfair.

Once in America, we drafted a constitution, then a bill of rights that later included the Equal Protection Clause, a provision unique to American law. When the Senate passed the amendment, the intent was to prevent discrimination against African Americans. But a nation obsessed with fairness for everyone soon saw the clause extended, among other things, to white applicants to law schools and, at one famous extreme, to small-town liquor-store owners in New Jersey who are treated differently than other New Jersey liquor-store owners.

We say life is unfair but then rebel against it; we think unfairness should be illegal. Often, our courts agree.

But what does this have to do with $30? To answer that, consider what goes through the heads of the shoppers in each of these hypotheticals.

If a watch costs $70 in Target and $40 three blocks away, we conceive of two possible explanations:

The store just blocks away is offering an incredible deal, or Target is gouging us. It's charging 75 percent more for that watch.

We don't apply this same thinking to the Samsung stereo. We decide that $800 is a fair price, just a couple percentage points higher than the other store's price. That marginally higher price may reflect Target's added overhead costs of more lighting, wider aisles, and sixteen checkout lanes and clerks. It's a fair price.

Something else works on our minds here: our sense of self. We'd feel foolish to avoid saving 75 percent on a single item; we'd be wasting money and cheating ourselves and our families not to take it. On top of that, a 75-percent savings represents treasure in the game of treasure hunt; we have to win that game.

But by contrast, is it imprudent for us to resist the 3.7-percent savings on the stereo? Is 3.7 percent off a treasure? Over the course of a year, if we spent $5,000 on discretionary purchases like the stereo, a 3.7-percent savings would equal $185—for which we'd have to walk several miles. If we spent $5,000 in discretionary purchases like the watch, however, over a year we'd save $3,750—*2,000 percent more.*

We *have* to take the watch deal—just like we have to give Kings of Leon a dollar for that song.

Our Wish to Stand Apart

When Burger King, which opened in 1954, begat McDonald's in 1955, we might have assumed there was little room left in the American drive-up burger business. But a company started even before them, in 1948, maintains a fanatical following in the West, partly by making each of its patrons feel like part of a special club.

The restaurants, In-N-Out Burger, claim distinction with their famous secret menu. Naturally, it's not printed but passed on by word of mouth from patron to devoted patron: the Flying Dutchman, the X times Y, the Fries American Style, for example. The founders of this quirky chain—the cups and burger wrappers are inscribed with citations to Bible passages—never discussed creating a secret menu. Their simple idea was to list on the menu only three burgers—the Double-Double, Hamburger, and Cheeseburger—but allow guests to have their burgers prepared any way they wished. It was the guests who coined the "secret menu" term, for the obvious reason that it made those who knew the details of it feel special.

Or perhaps we should say fanatical. When a new In-N-Out opened in Scottsdale, Arizona, in 2002, local news helicopters hovered over the parking lot and captured a remarkable image: the lines. At one point, the wait for food was four hours.

Tattoos, Nightsters, and Design-Us-Ourselves

Starting after the Second World War, tattoos were regarded as the signal of a former Navy man who one night had been mightily overserved in a bar next to a tattoo parlor. Soon thereafter, tattoos also became identified with the Hells Angels and other rebel gangs, and later with gangstas and NBA basketball players, who without them would all be uniformly attired, literally; their tattoos alone set them apart.

Today, you see tattoos everywhere. (This writer's four-leaf clover, with his children's initials, HWCC, is on the inside of his left bicep, nearest his heart.) Thirty-six percent of Americans between ages eighteen and twenty-nine—more than one in three—wears at least one. A typical Barnes & Noble displays more tattoo publications (eleven) than parenting magazines. Two networks currently feature tattoo programs: A&E's *Inked* and The Learning Channel's *Miami Ink* and *LA Ink*.

Tattoos are us.

What does a tattoo say? A tattoo is a logo, except that the logo we wear—Polos or Abercrombies—tells us what group we belong to and perhaps signals our disposable income.

A tattoo is a logo for a person. It brands us unlike any other person, and yet, being relatively common, also conveys that we are a part, too, of the huge community of fellow wearers. Perhaps more important, it tells the wearer something every day, too: In this incredibly crowded world, it assures the wearer, "You are special."

Today, we can set ourselves apart by designing what we own.

At NikeiD, a vivid example of one shrewd marketer's recognition of Apart, we can click on a basic Nike shoe style and then make it our own.

Take, for one entertaining example, the $102 Nike Zoom T-5 iD Boot. (For added entertainment, enter "harryb" in the search box, check "Catsup, meet mustard," then redesign that red and yellow iD Boot so it looks much better to your eye—and sets you apart.)

We can choose either a flat-bottomed sole or a rubber-studded sole for more traction; we can choose five colors for the outside base, five for the inside base, and five others for the inside eye stay; we can choose three colors for the tip, nine for the collar around the ankle, and nine others for the heel. When we're done, we can add words, say our name, in any of eleven colors, one word on the tongue, and a different one at the top of each of the arches.

Doing the math, we learn we can make 6,743,250 versions of the iD Boot even before we inscribe it with any words we choose. Nike gets it: We want to set ourselves apart.

Harley-Davidson understands our desire to feel apart, too. For years, a motorcycle was a motorcycle, to which you could later add accessories, such as leather saddlebags.

But the people at Harley soon realized that most Harley owners wanted unique motorcycles, and the way to provide them was not with options but accessories: not just one or two saddlebags but perhaps a hundred, and not just saddlebags but different bars and grips, foot pegs and floorboards, exhausts, seats, sissy bars, luggage racks, windshields, body parts, wheels and tires.

Buy a Harley, then design the Harley: Set yourself apart.

In 2007, Harley-Davidson introduced a new version of its Nightster. Fans immediately sensed something different about it, but few of them could figure it out. What was it?

The license plate was hung to the left of the rear

fender, not in the center. Why? "I wanted people to wonder if it was legal," says designer Rich Christoph. He wanted Nightster drivers to have that feeling of pushing the limits, of Easy Riding with Fonda and Hopper to Mardi Gras, or of being Brando in *The Wild One*. Rich Christoph knows we rooted for Bonnie and Clyde. And that we want to stand apart.

Public and private companies weren't the first marketers to recognize that vehicle owners could use license plates to set themselves apart. Almost seventy years ago, the state of Pennsylvania introduced America's first vanity plates, on which drivers could inscribe whatever inoffensive combination of seven letters and numbers they wished.

Today we see vanity plates everywhere, sometimes an unusual one that merely repeats what we already know: the brand of the car. A few others might be considered unsafe, however, because our spasms of laughter might cause us to veer off the road. These include the white Ford Bronco plate that reads "Not OJ," the Hummer with the plate "1 MPG," and the Acura NSX—a car that can reach 165 miles per hour—with the plate "NVR L8."

And there's the one that stops traffic daily. Imagine yourself in downtown Lexington, Kentucky, pulling up behind a black hearse, looking down to its license plate, and reading this: "U R NXT."

The Rise and Fall of Krispy Kreme

On June 10, 2002, *The New York Times* reported that Krispy Kreme doughnuts had earned "a fan following to make any corporate branding agent proud." That following and the brand looked so strong that a year later, on April 11, 2003, the stock ended the day trading for almost $489 a share. A person who had bought Krispy Kreme stock exactly three years earlier had watched it soar almost 480 percent.

Krispy Kreme was rocketing.

But let's say you decided on that same day, April 11, 2003, that Krispy Kreme *was* rocketing, that its fans were so loyal and its brand so compelling that you had to buy the stock. What if on that rollicking day you had bought $10,000 in Krispy Kreme stock?

Be glad you didn't.

Today as this is being written, your $10,000 investment in Krispy Kreme stock would be worth $620. *Six hundred and twenty dollars.*

We might assume Krispy Kreme merely fell with the market. That's not the explanation. The Dow Jones Industrial Average since the day you made your hypothetical $10,000 investment has risen 8 percent.

What happened here? Any steep fall takes several pushes. Most analysts agree the company got too ambitious, perhaps even greedy, as *CFO* magazine suggested in 2005. They agree that the company managed its franchisees poorly, as one might expect from a company with no experience in franchising.

We may also speculate that Americans had become more health and calorie conscious, and that low-carb diets like the Atkins Diet helped kill Krispy Kreme. But that cannot be the explanation, even though Krispy Kreme executives offered that excuse when the nosedive began. The Atkins Diet was introduced thirty years earlier, and in the year Krispy Kreme's stock started free-falling, Dr. Atkins died, which set off rumors that his low-carb diet had contributed to his death.

So where should we look for the fall of these yeast-raised doughnuts? Let's start with that *New York Times* article and that "fan following."

Krispy Kreme's executives made a critical error. They assumed that what people loved about Krispy Kreme was its "sweet and impossibly fluffy" doughnuts, as the company proudly describes them. There was much more to its appeal.

Consider this common street scene in 2003, near Central Park in New York City.

Man spots two twentysomethings munching doughnuts ecstatically. The girl is holding a white, red, and green Krispy Kreme bag.

"Hey, sorry, but where'd you get those Krispy Kremes?"

"Over near Penn Station, around Thirty-second."

"Hey, are they as delicious as everybody says?"

"Oh man, yes, it was *so* worth the walk! Head down there!"

In the man's position, you would have done what he did: Hike twenty-five blocks, stand in line, and buy six doughnuts that were gone by the next morning.

That was 2003. Then Krispy Kreme decided to make doughnut lovers' lives easier by distributing their treats everywhere. Soon, we could find Krispy Kremes at Target and at convenience stores like SuperAmerica. At long last, we could get Krispy Kremes in the same places we could score a 99-cent shrink-wrapped ham-and-cheese sandwich!

Krispy Kreme's appeal when it was small and hard to find was just that: the doughnuts were hard to get, which made them a cult item. A search for Krispy Kremes was a treasure hunt, like finding the super deals at Costco and knowing where to find them was like knowing the secret menu at In-N-Out Burger.

We value things that are hard to find; they strike us as special and seem more valuable. As Tom Vanderbilt points out in *Traffic,* we leave great parking spots slowly for that reason; the spot was hard to find, so we are slower to give it up. We coveted James Bond's girls for the same reason; they always played hard to get.

And Krispy Kreme's game had been hard to get.

The company thought we loved Krispy Kreme doughnuts, but we didn't. We loved the *idea* of Krispy Kreme doughnuts. We weren't buying a snack; we were buying a find, a cult item, a treasure hunt, the pleasure of appearing to be in-the-know. Hard-to-get Krispy Kremes tasted great; Krispy Kremes from a store where we could get shrink-wrapped ham-and-cheese sandwiches represented another idea entirely.

And we didn't buy that idea.

The Age of Me: Talking to Us

Seeing our self-absorption has led American marketers to an obvious tactic right out of Brian Epstein's playbook: Enough about our products! *Let's talk about you.*

Try this: Visit Nike.com. Scan down to the first row of images. At this writing, they are for Nike-Store, and what words immediately follow that? "Gear Up for *Your* Sport." Scan over to the third item in the top row, and you see "Nike+." And what appears next in that box? "Run for *Your* Sport."

Nike captured its essence by not talking about itself at all, nor even its products. Instead, it merely talked to us and our desires. It encouraged us to "Just do it." It was talking to each of us.

Very soon, the You wave turned into a tsunami. In August 2003, several Californians captured the You spirit with a social networking site aptly called MySpace. By 2006 it had become the world's most popular networking site. In February 2005, three former employees of PayPal launched a site to host videos online: YouTube.

Always alert to trends, the editors of *Time* magazine were then considering naming their Person of the Year. Months later, the magazine, which in past years had given that honor three times to Franklin D. Roosevelt and twice to Winston Churchill, made a fitting choice for the Me Century.

They named each of us the 2006 Person of the Year. They chose "You."

As with most things, if some is good, lots is better. Now everyone talks just to us, as if we're the only people in the room. It's typified in the best-selling success of *You: The Owner's Manual,* a book just about each of us. The winter of the year that *You* first appeared, fans of then-Green Bay Packer quarterback Brett Favre received a treat when ABC's *Monday Night Football* aired a short tribute film. It concluded with his wife's memorable words: "My Brett. Our Favre."

Brett Favre was ours, too.

In 2009, motorists in Minnesota were treated to the Me Century's most extreme manifestation, a billboard fourteen steps east of the entrance to the Minikahda Club. It captured the Me Century perfectly, showing a woman apparently uttering the words: MY CANCER. MY WORKOUTS. MY FAIRVIEW.

In the first weeks of February of the very next year, Minnesotans driving west on that road experienced profound déjà vu when they sensed that the billboard had been replaced, as they read this new one: MY POP CULTURE. MY MUSIC. MY RADIO STATION. MY TALK 107.1.

Today, what do we have? We have My FootJoys, My Excite, My Flickr, My T-Mobile, My Yahoo!, My Coke Rewards, My Starbucks Idea, My MSN, MyTV (anticipated by MTV's perceptive slogan, "I Want My MTV"). We have My after My after My. Everyone is talking just to us and making everything just for each of us alone.

The wonderfully popular American writer Malcolm Gladwell understands our self-preoccupation, too. Check out these excerpts from his fine book *Outliers* and see what you see.

"Over the course of the chapters ahead, I'm going to introduce you to one kind of outlier...."

"What is the question we always ask about the successful?"

"Look back at the Medicine Hat roster. Do you see it now?"

As Gladwell himself would now write: *What did you just notice?*

He is writing to each of us, even asking us questions not just like a good writer but like something we treasure far more: a good listener. (The wit Fran Lebowitz once captured our preoccupation with talking by noting, "The opposite of talking isn't listening. It's waiting.")

Gladwell talks to us and seems to listen to us. He knows this is the Me Century, when everyone who passes by a television camera waves in the hope of being noticed. Gladwell crafts his books with that knowledge, and we buy them by the millions.

We want everything—our golf shoes, our running shoes, our coffee shops, our TV shows—to be about us. The best marketers, including many of our most popular authors, make sure that it is.

II. We: The Great Togetherists

———

American Gothic, Chris Isaak, and *Cast Away*

One sunny afternoon in 1930, a painter driving through Eldon, Iowa, spotted a house that appealed to him. He pictured who might live in the house and, after imagining them, sought out two models to portray them.

He knew the perfect woman. His thirty-year-old sister, Nan, looked just like the woman the painter had imagined. To pose as her husband, the painter made the unusual choice of a man more than twice Nan's age: Byron McKeeby, a sixty-three-year-old from Cedar Rapids who for years had been the painter's dentist.

The painting that resulted, showing a somber, bald farmer holding a pitchfork while the farmer's wife stares vacantly to her left, became Grant Wood's iconic American painting *American Gothic*.

Almost sixty years before, James Whistler had painted what became our country's first iconic painting. It portrays a white-haired mother staring grimly to our left as we view it, a vision so cold and spare that its original title, *Study in Black and White*, seems apt. We know this classic painting well, however, by its other title: *Whistler's Mother*.

Eighteen years after *American Gothic* was created, Andrew Wyeth painted what became our country's third iconic work. It depicts a woman lying in a vast field of wispy golden grass, staring toward a weathered farmhouse in the distant background. Her slumped body suggests that she may be too weak to walk to the farmhouse and whatever comfort it might offer. This painting, *Christina's World*, is the second-most reproduced American painting of all time and helped make Wyeth among our richest painters. In 2006, another austere Wyeth painting, this of the interior of a farmhouse living room, fetched $4.4 million at an auction.

Is it the artistry that makes these three paintings iconic? It doesn't appear that way. In a recent *New York Times* poll of the twentieth century's greatest artists, two hundred men and women, including twenty-five Americans, earned votes, but neither Wood nor Wyeth was among them.

So if it's not the artistry of these three works, why have we embraced them as our icons? Look long at the three—of Christina, of the couple in *American Gothic,* and of Whistler's mother—and you will feel it: *These four people look utterly alone.*

The bald farmer stands by his wife but looks miles away emotionally; she cannot look at the person painting her. Christina sits far from the farmhouse, seemingly unable to rise to walk to the house, and it appears the house would offer her no comfort once she got there: It looks deserted. Whistler's mother looks frozen in her chair, deserted and solemn.

What might these paintings say about us? Researchers of phobias have learned that Americans do not list snakes, spiders, or the dark as their fears. They say one thing scares us most: the thought of being alone.

In the weeks following Michael Jackson's death in June 2009, few commentators mentioned, and few fans remembered, that Jackson's most phenomenal success was a song that expressed his view: We are all in this together.

"We Are the World," which Jackson cowrote with Quincy Jones to raise money for African famine relief, was the fastest-selling pop single in American history, the country's first multiplatinum single, and a winner of three Grammy Awards. (It's possible that so many forget the song because so few singers liked it. At one point in rehearsals, Cyndi Lauper leaned forward and whispered to Bruce Springsteen, "It sounds like a Pepsi commercial." The Boss whispered back, "I can't disagree.")

We hear it in our music: We want to be a part and dread being alone.

In 2004, the editors of *Rolling Stone* polled Slash, k.d. lang, members of the Ramones and No Doubt, and more than one hundred other insiders for their year-end issue on the five hundred greatest songs of all time. The voters' top choice was Bob Dylan's "Like a Rolling Stone," about a character called Miss Lonely and with a title derived from the Hank Williams verse. "I'm a rolling stone, I'm lost and alone":

How does it feel
To be on your own
With no direction home
Like a complete unknown?

Rolling Stone's voters had dozens of classic lonely songs to choose from: Williams' "I'm So Lonesome I Could Cry"; Roy Orbison's "Only the Lonely"; Jackie Wilson's "Lonely Teardrops"; Elvis Presley's "Are You

Lonesome Tonight?"; the Beatles' "Help!" (the number-one song when Dylan's song reached its peak at number two) and "all the lonely people" in "Eleanor Rigby"; Presley's "Heartbreak Hotel" on "Lonesome Street," covered later by Lynyrd Skynyrd and Guns N' Roses; and the Righteous Brothers' "Unchained Melody," covered by U2 and LeAnn Rimes.

The singer Chris Isaak actually made a career obsessing on this subject: "Seven Lonely Nights," "Only the Lonely," "Lonely with a Broken Heart," and "The Lonely Ones," plus "The Blue Hotel" and "Nothing to Say."

Our three iconic paintings and numerous popular songs seem to express our greatest dread and strongest need: We dread loneliness and want to be a part.

We see this in our movies, too. In 2007's *Lars and the Real Girl,* Lars lives in a garage and emerges from his loneliness only for work and the rare nights when his brother succeeds in persuading Lars to come for dinner.

On one of those days, Lars accepts the invitation and adds that he will be bringing a friend. His brother looks thrilled.

That night, Lars appears and introduces the friend, Bianca. She is confined to a wheelchair but has a more conspicuous handicap: She's a plastic sex doll.

The two fall in love, and others come to love the couple, too. This story sounds silly at best, revolting at worst, and impossible to turn into a movie that people could tolerate, much less enjoy. But among other enthusiastic critics, Kenneth Turan of the *Los Angeles Times* called it "the sweetest, most inno-cent, most completely enjoyable movie around," as it traces Lars's escape from loneliness.

The romance of Lars and Bianca resembles another memorable screen friendship. In *Cast Away*, a FedEx plane crashes and strands a Wilson volleyball and a character played by Tom Hanks on an island. The two become friends; Hanks calls him Wilson.

In their weeks together, Hanks's affection for Wilson deepens so much that at a climactic point, he risks his life swimming through rough surf to rescue his round friend. Again, what happened to the audiences? They were touched.

We dread being alone; we want to be a part.

We started out that way, it appears. Check briefly this observation by one of America's best-known early authors, James Fenimore Cooper, who wrote *Leatherstocking Tales*:

In England a man dines by himself in a room filled with other hermits, he eats at his lei-sure, drinks his wine in silence, reads the paper by the hour; the American is compelled to submit to a common rule; he eats when others eat, sleeps when others sleep, and he is lucky, indeed, if he can read a paper in a tavern without having a stranger looking over each shoulder.

We Are the World

Less than 59 minutes after midnight on Christmas 2004, the longest-lasting and second-largest earthquake ever recorded occurred off the west coast of Sumatra, Indonesia. Its most memorable and devastating effect was to produce a series of tsunamis, some with waves that reached 100 feet high. When these waves touched land, they shredded it. Nearly 230,000 people in fourteen countries died as a result.

The impact was felt in America; the entire planet actually shook. And in the days and months that followed, we watched for hours on television, grieved the losses, sent money, and even flew to countries affected to help them rebuild.

The actor George Clooney immediately went to work, too. Inspired by the many aid events, beginning with the famous 1985 Live Aid concert that raised $284 million for famine relief in Ethiopia,

Clooney in just two weeks arranged *Tsunami Aid: A Concert of Hope,* which aired on NBC and its affiliated networks and raised $5 million for the relief effort. Americans gave an estimated $13 million more, and the U.S. government gave countries in the region over $350 million, plus military and logistical help with rebuilding.

When outsiders criticize Americans, they regularly note that we seem self-centered, which we are. But few contend we are selfish, and with good reason; we are not. Every international need organization knows that to market its cause—cleft palates, tsunamis in Indonesia, or needy Romanian orphans, to name three—they need to go to America first.

One could argue that there was little need to call on many Americans after the tsunami, because many of us would not answer; we already had booked our tickets to Indonesia.

We are compassionate, and it ties strongly to this theme: our striving for community and our need of others. You see this in the words "compassion" and "community." They share the root *com,* which comes from the Latin word for "together." When you think about the word "passion," you may immediately think of a favorite image of romantic passion, but surprise: "passion" comes from the Latin *pati* and means "to suffer." "Compassion" literally means "suffering with." And as exemplified by our

Marshall Plan to restore Europe after World War II and our Peace Corps to restore much of the world during the Kennedy administration, no one "suffers with" others like Americans.

This helps explain the effectiveness of cause-based marketing in America, reflected in the decades-long cause advertising of Kenneth Cole, the Red promotion by the Gap and others in the mid-2000s, the "share good fortune" cause promoted by Tazo on all its tea packages, and the bandwagon that is the green movement today.

At its root, might our wanting to be a part be the force at work? To take part in a cause is to be a part of something bigger, and fortunately for unfortunate people here and everywhere else in the world, no people suffer with others as passionately as we do.

Tall, Dark, and Handsome? The Lesson of American Actors

Scan this list of the ten highest-earning actors of 2008. Then ask, "What do these men have in common?"

1. Harrison Ford
2. Adam Sandler

3. Will Smith
4. Eddie Murphy
5. Nicholas Cage
6. Tom Hanks
7. Tom Cruise
8. Jim Carrey
9. Brad Pitt
10. George Clooney

To make the list comprise all the leading actors of our decade, let's add the 2008 Academy Award winner for best actor, Sean Penn; plus Matt Damon, Robert DeNiro, Al Pacino, Dustin Hoffman, and America's two hottest actors, Leonardo DiCaprio and Johnny Depp.

Now, let's step back briefly.

Whenever we hear the expression "leading man," we probably think of that classic description: "tall, dark, and handsome."

But who among those actors fits that description? Sandler, Murphy, and Carrey perform in comedies and not as standard dramatic leading men. Harrison Ford comes closest to TD&H, but he's not dark. While undeniably dark and handsome, Clooney stands barely 5 feet 10 inches, eye level with Depp and Richard Gere—and with Sandler and Murphy.

The only actor on our seventeen-man list over

6 feet tall is Cage, who few would call dark or handsome, even during the years when he sported more hair. Pitt barely hits 6 feet, above average but only arguably tall—and definitely not dark.

America's leading men are not tall. They're short. DeNiro stands 5 feet 9 inches, Pacino 5 feet 8 inches, and the great American actor of his generation, Marlon Brando, topped out at 5 feet 9 inches. Yet that's a full inch taller than Mel Gibson and two inches taller than the 5-feet-7-inch Sylvester Stallone.

Michael Douglas, Paul Newman, James Dean? 5 feet 9 inches. Damon? An eyebrow taller. Penn? 5 feet 8 inches. The undeniably dark and handsome Tom Cruise? He's 5 feet 8 inches, too.

What might account for this "fairly short, often dark, mostly handsome" trend? Does it suggest that we prefer our movie stars to be like us and that we don't want to be looked down on, literally or figuratively?

Consider how television shows have been cast. The classic popular quiz shows hosts Bill Cullen, Garry Moore, and Allen Ludden worked constantly. Moore and Cullen sported goofy crew cuts, Ludden and Cullen wore thick glasses, and Moore wore bow ties at a time when the cooler guys didn't.

Move on to John Goodman, Jerry Seinfeld and Kramer and George, Larry David, Drew Carey, and on and on. The classic TV show of our decade may be *Survivor,* now in its twenty-second season, each hosted by the dark and undeniably handsome Jeff Probst—all 5 feet 9 inches of him. He's the same height as Howie Mandel, host of the once-popular quiz show *Deal or No Deal,* and an inch taller than Alex Trebek of the classic quiz show *Jeopardy!* now in its forty-seventh year.

What television star has been on camera more than any other? At 16,400 hours and counting—the *Guinness Book of World Records* did the counting—it's Regis Philbin, host of *Live with Regis and Kelly* and former host of the hit *Who Wants to Be a Millionaire,* who has the record. He's 5 feet 7 inches.

Look again at the Apple computer ads and the likable but not tall, dark, or handsome chill kid played by Justin Long.

The often-repeated old compliment "You look like a movie star" seems bizarre today. If you want to be in movies, the person you really should look like is the friendly Joe next door. Just ask superstar actor next door Tom Hanks, who admits to being the nerd of his Oakland, California, high school class.

Contrast our popular actors with England's: Laurence Olivier, John Gielgud, and Alec Guinness. Each projected a quality that doesn't work on American audiences, who believe all of us are equal. These Brits oozed self-regard—conceit, really. Gielgud was so skilled at condescension that director Steve

Gordon cast him as Dudley Moore's snooty butler in *Arthur,* and Guinness projected the needed air of superiority required for the role of Obi-Wan Kenobi in *Star Wars.* The very un-American air of these Brits is suggested by their titles: Each is a sir, a title bestowed by the British Crown.

Could the contrast between us and the English be greater? British actors belong to royalty; our actors belong to us. They make us feel a part of them.

Americans love celebrity gossip. Gossip brings hot shots down to our level, even tosses them below it. We hear that these mortals abuse drugs (Robert Downey, Jr.), stalk other stars (Sean Young), punch out photographers (Sean Penn), punch out everyone (model Naomi Campbell), or do all of this (Britney Spears and Lindsay Lohan). We read that they cheat on lovers and spouses with pathological frequency. The famous act just like us, only worse.

America's agents work overtime bringing their clients down to us. That's almost certainly why Pitt dresses down, affecting goofy porkpie hats and a wardrobe that suggests his total unawareness of the merits of color draping. Cage and Kevin Spacey seem to lose more hair with every film. Jack Nicholson goes bald and fat and does nothing to hide it.

Our stars are just like us.

Which raises the question: Whatever happened

to toupees? Sean Connery sported one for years, faded from view, then resurrected his post–James Bond career after he ditched his hairpiece. You could argue he did this for a simple reason: he had to. At 6 feet 2 inches, Connery was the last truly tall, dark, and handsome popular actor of the last thirty years. He had to knock himself down a few notches, down here with us. So he did.

Yes, we like tall, dark, and handsome presidents. But our presidents are, among other things, the commanders in chief of our armed forces. So we want people who fit that description: *commanding*. That means big, forceful, someone who could stare down Nikita Khrushchev, Saddam Hussein, or Osama bin Laden. That's why Michael Dukakis's operatives stuck him in a tank for a famous photo-op and George Bush's showed him off in fighter-pilot garb for yet another one. We want our actors to make us feel good; we want our presidents to make us feel safe.

"I'm one of you," our actors assure us. "I may look handsome, but I'm short. I am not Will Ferrell but a guy who removes his shirt to show off my 40-inch paunch hanging over badly fitting shorts." Ferrell and Vince Vaughn win huge audiences by making fun of themselves, a solution to their acting handicaps: Ferrell is 6 feet 3 inches, and Vaughn is

6 feet 5 inches. If they didn't put themselves down, we'd feel dwarfed by them. Hence the expression "put oneself down," back here with us.

"Don't take us seriously," our tallest actors tell us. "We may be bigger, but we're just like you—and all those not-tall actors you love so much."

We're one of you.

The American Way: Trust None of Us But All of Us

A visitor to America today could not be here long without recognizing an American obsession: bestseller lists.

Every week, *USA Today* and other publications alert Americans to which movies attracted the most viewers, all the way down to movie number ten. Each week, it lists not just the ten best-selling books but the top one hundred. Meanwhile, newspapers each week inform us of the most popular television shows, CDs, country music songs. Amazon provides constantly updated lists of its best-selling books, right down to number 3,500,000.

But of course we care about this. We badly want to know what everyone else is doing and to feel a part of it.

Perhaps we are wise to think this way, to watch what others are doing and thinking. As James Surowiecki pointed out in his 2003 book *The Wisdom of Crowds,* the masses often act intelligently.

When contestants on the television program *Who Wants to Be a Millionaire* asked for help from the "smartest person" they knew, those smart people provided the right answer almost 65 percent of the time. That was a strong performance, but far less impressive than the people in the audience; they picked the right answer 91 percent of the time; the consensus of the audience proved almost 40-percent smarter than the smartest person each contestant knew.

Standing by itself, the *Millionaire* example doesn't prove Surowiecki's theory, well expressed in his book's subtitle, *Why the Many Are Smarter Than the Few.* But he assembles several other examples to suggest how often experts are wrong—we will see many examples in the pages ahead—and crowds are right.

Which raises the possibility: Do we follow the crowd because we have learned that crowds know something? Is there simply something about that number-one movie, book, or television show that truly recommends it?

We trust the common view; no, we are obsessed with it. *USA Today* constantly publicizes its surveys, under headlines like "We Love Country Music" and "We're Watching More Television." We poll and poll and poll. One of our country's most popular sets of business books, Marcus Buckingham's, claims to be the product of Gallup polls of more than 1.7 million people. Implicitly, this assures us that his books offer the "wisdom of crowds."

We want to know what people are reading and watching because we want to participate in the dialogue about those shows and books. Just as significant, we do not want to feel left out of those conversations. We want to be a part.

Great marketers tap into this tendency, too. Consider Roger Horchow, who for years has engineered one of the world's most successful catalog businesses, the Horchow Catalog. A reader browsing his catalog would soon be attracted to a teak desk set and a Danish brass kitchen clock. Very often, the reason for her interest is that she's discovered that other people like those two items, too. How does she know? Roger told her. He used his three magic words, which appear throughout his catalog: "Our most popular."

"This is what others are buying," Horchow tells a reader with those three words, and the reader reacts like Americans so often do: "I'd better buy it, too."

Following the Crowds Over the Cliffs to the Malls: 2008–2010

Beginning just after Thanksgiving Day in 1995, when it first surpassed the 5,000 mark, the Dow Jones Industrial Average, which tracks the stock performance of thirty blue-chip companies, more than doubled in just over three years. In March 1999, it reached 11,000. By 2000, the market's performance had been gasp-inducing: a 315-percent increase in just ten years, almost triple its average increase.

After some notable drops, including a 1,360-point drop in the week following September 11, stocks broke the 11,000 level again on January 9, 2006, then started rising almost vertically. In less than seven months, the Dow hit 14,164.

Everyone recognized this was extraordinary, but too few people recognized it could not last. American stocks had increased an average of just over 10 percent per year for the previous one hundred years. A 125-percent increase in a decade would fit that norm; this 315-percent burst did not.

Each day, CNN and others offered reasons for the surge: strong performance from the tech sector, continued good news on inflation, and investor confidence in Federal Reserve chairman Alan Greenspan. They never offered another explanation, which seems far more plausible now: People were buying stocks *because people were buying stocks.*

Jon and Dawn bought stocks because Kim and Cliff and Kevin and Julie and everyone else seemed to be buying stocks, and they wanted to be a part. Consider what Jon and Dawn had been enduring. For weeks, they'd indulged several friends who raved about their brokers and their own investing acumen, which had helped steer their portfolio up 40 percent. Like most of us, Jon and Dawn can endure one of these conversations, but few among us can endure three—and at various times between 1996 and 2001, most investors had.

America's financial advisors constantly heard this. "My friend David has made a real killing in Pfizer," Jon would tell them. "The Browns made so much last year that Eva quit her job," Dawn would chime in. And on and on. Everyone was looking at everyone.

This was their problem. David, Eva, and everyone else seemed to be making huge sums of money. Jon and Dawn didn't want to get further ahead; they simply did not want to fall behind. They did not want to lose their place.

When the market and economy reversed, they still showed the passion; they just moved to another venue. In the middle of June 2009 and a hideous recession, we could head for the nearest mall and detect a pleasant feeling. We knew we would get a great parking spot, right near the entrance, because surely people weren't shopping.

We drove in. Not an empty slot. We decided it was an odd day, perhaps a huge sale.

But it wasn't. Mall traffic throughout the summer of 2009 was virtually unchanged from traffic levels of the peak years.

We really were still shopping.

If we weren't at the mall, we were communing with crowds at another venue. Despite the bleak economy in 2009, four teams—Michigan, Penn State, Tennessee, and Texas—once again attracted more than 100,000 fans to each of its home games, and the average Division I team attracted over 42,000.

We can see the communal nature of these sports when we watch how they are televised. Watch when one team makes a big play; the camera almost instantly goes to the crowd to watch its joyous reaction, en masse. The camera watches the game; but like us, it watches the crowd to see if it's cheering, shopping, or buying stock.

We want to be a part.

The Hog's Wonderful Tale: CAAS

In 1973, Harley-Davidson claimed near-monopoly status in the United States, a phenomenal 77.5 percent of the motorcycle market. The brand was iconic and was made even more so by the classic 1969 movie *Easy Rider,* which launched the celebrated careers of Jack Nicholson and Dennis Hopper, showcasing Wyatt (Peter Fonda) and Bill (Hopper) on two Harley choppers, going from Los Angeles to Mardi Gras in search of America.

But in 1973, from its stronghold in Milwaukee, Harley came under attack from Japan: from Yamaha, Honda, Suzuki, and the other manufacturers of much lighter, hyperpowered motorcycles. Owners of aptly named Hogs—a Harley weighed far more than a comparable Yamaha—stayed famously true to their enormous bikes, but young American men gravitated to these Japanese crotch rockets, partly because they were bikes young men could afford.

The lower-cost Japanese bikes dramatically altered the market by dramatically expanding it. As a result, Harley started bleeding. Ten years later, its market share had plummeted to just one bike in four on America's roads. Almost half of the bikes on the road, an amazing 44 percent, were Hondas.

Honda did it, some might argue, through sheer

bitchiness manifested in shrewd marketing. Honda decided to make Harley look bad, and it had plenty of ammunition, thanks to a series of unfortunate events.

Early in 1969, seeing the enormous success of the famous Woodstock concert, the group Crosby, Stills, Nash & Young decided they wanted to create a West Coast version to celebrate the end of the year. They quickly signed two of the era's most famous rock groups: Santana and Jefferson Airplane. They then guaranteed a massive crowd. They signed the Rolling Stones.

But the Rolling Stones could not appear in the proposed setting without first enlisting heavy security. In what seemed a fortunate coincidence, they learned that the concert site was near the birthplace of a perfect security organization: the Hells Angels. The Stones' leader, Mick Jagger, had earlier hired some London-based Angels to provide security for a concert in London and was happy with their performance.

But the English Angels, he would later learn, were a more angelic band than the Americans he approached.

A small group of motorcycle-riding outlaws that officially started in 1948 near Oakland, California, the Angels had a violent image in America that dated to the previous summer and a famous event: the

Fourth of July riot in Hollister, California. The riot immediately became known for the headline it inspired in the *San Francisco Chronicle* the following morning: "70 Motorcyclists Take Over Town."

Always eager for sensational stories that photographed well, *Life* magazine photographers got to the scene, gathered dozens of beer bottles, and asked one of the riders still in Hollister to pose on his motorcycle in the midst of bottles while holding another bottle to his mouth. To take full advantage of readers' interest, *Life*'s story ran over 1,500 words.

That vivid photo and lengthy coverage branded in Americans' minds the image of motorcyclists as deviant, drunken outlaws. Less than four years later, *Harper's* ran a story called "Cyclists Raid" based on the *Life* story. Reading the story and immediately seeing its cinematic potential, *Harper's* subscriber and movie director Stanley Kramer set into motion the steps that two years later produced the classic movie *The Wild One,* starring Marlon Brando.

Kramer's movie started a cult of motorcycle gang films. *Life*'s editors years later admitted they had created the image of outlaw motorcyclists that motorcyclists had been trying to live down ever since. And the group most associated with that outlaw image was the Hells Angels.

Mick Jagger, however, did not subscribe to *Life* or

Harper's. He knew nothing about Hollister; when the riot occurred, he was three weeks shy of five years old and living in London. Jagger simply assumed—once again, a triumph of assuming over thinking—that America's Angels were like the English Angels he'd liked and trusted. They weren't. The British Angels looked remarkably like Jagger: thin, long-haired, often androgynous, and nonviolent.

So a deal was struck to have the Angels provide security: They'd do it for $500 worth of beer.

Everything now seemed in place to make Altamont the next Woodstock, a festival salute to peace, love, and rock and roll.

But from the beginning, it wasn't. The day, December 6, 1969, started ominously. Two people died after being struck by a hit-and-run driver, and a third person drowned in a puddle of water, which caused some audience members to challenge the fitness of the Angels as guards.

In midafternoon, a helicopter hovered dramatically over the Altamont Speedway before fluttering down. The Stones broke out the helicopter's door and rushed to the stage. By that point, everyone could feel the tension between the Angels and the crowd. To make matters worse, someone knocked over one of the Angels' bikes. Soon after, one of the Angels knocked out Jefferson Airplane's Marty

Balin with a punch, the last straw for Crosby, Stills, Nash & Young. The group that created the concert left the speedway.

Unfortunately, bad got worse. The Stones' bassist Bill Wyman had missed the helicopter ride, so the Stones had to wait to perform. It was dark before they finally started, and Jagger's justifiable edginess is vivid in the footage in the documentary *Gimme Shelter*. It is hard not to notice something else that was contributing to the tension: The Angels were well through their $500 cache of beer.

About twenty minutes later, as the Stones performed their classic "Under My Thumb," an eighteen-year-old man near the front of the stage pulled out a gun and what some thought was a knife. He approached the stage, wild-eyed and barely able to walk.

Spotting the man and his gun, several Angels surged into the crowd. One Angel, Alan Passaro, fended off the gunman with his left hand and stabbed him with a knife he held in his right. Jagger stopped singing and watched anxiously, a moment powerfully captured in *Gimme Shelter,* which was released just months later.

The Stones continued and finished the set, unaware of the news: Meredith Hunter had died from the wounds inflicted by the Angels. Passaro later would be charged with murder but then acquitted after lawyers successfully argued that he had acted in self-defense.

But after that December and the release of the documentary, the Angels' devotion to Harley made them the most vivid image of the Harley brand, which at that point was equated with Altamont and its horror. To make the connection even worse was something viewers realize when they see *Gimme Shelter*: All of the performers and the Angels were white. Meredith Hunter was black.

Honda's marketing executives spotted this monumental event—it is popular to call Woodstock the high point of "the culture of love" and Altamont its violent end—as an opportunity. They could turn Harley's new problem into Harley's new catastrophe and a launchpad for Honda. Honda's advertising agency, Daly and Associates, went to work and soon made a weapon.

They crafted a velvet hammer.

Their weapon was eight words, of such apparent innocence that they might have been used in a Pepsi commercial. The message sounded so sweet, so like "I'd like to buy the world a Coke," that most people who saw the commercial completely missed its intended meaning. What Honda and its agency wanted Americans to hear beneath these words' veneer was, "Don't buy a Harley, because a Harley rider might invade your hometown, pee on your jacket, and beat you to death with a pool cue."

That was what Honda's executives and ad agency hoped Americans would hear. What they said, however, was, "You meet the nicest people on a Honda."

And, by implication, you meet the biggest, scariest, pool-cue-wielding dudes on a Harley.

The message and Honda's dramatic rise forced the already-wounded Harley folks in Milwaukee to go on the defensive. Harley could not pretend there were no Hells Angels, in part because too many men found Harley's outlaw image attractive, in part because so many women did. Outlaws we like; cold-blooded, pool-cue-wielding killers we don't.

Realizing its motorcycles weren't as fast, agile, or affordable as the Japanese bikes, afraid to kill the Hog by making it into something smaller and less masculine, and forced into what seemed a brand hole, Harley had to respond. Rather than escape the tattooed Angels image, Harley embraced it, cleaned it up, and turned it—and Harley's uniquely passionate brand loyalty—into an asset.

Harley owners so loved their Harleys that tens of thousands had the Harley logo tattooed on their arms. That image became an inspiration, but one the company took years to recognize. Once it did, however, the effect was memorable.

In 1985, Harley's top creative team at Carmichael Lynch in Minneapolis, copywriter Ron Sackett and art director Dan Krumwiede, met and began to think about all those tattooed biceps.

Krumwiede envisioned the photo: a gorgeous close-up of a thick, bronzed bicep, popping out from below a spotless new white shirt, emblazoned with the Harley logo. Sackett thought about just what that meant, to love a brand so much you branded yourself with it, and crafted his "think about this, all you guys on those Japanese crotch rockets" headline: "When is the last time you felt this passionately about anything?"

But Harley's strongest rejoinder actually started two years before, when the Harley marketing teams recognized that great American trait: We want to be a part. This spurred the Milwaukee-Minneapolis team to come up with an audacious idea: What if we start a new motorcycle gang?

What if we created an even bigger gang and became more than just a motorcycle company but a collection of companions?

From that insight was born one of the most successful marketing tactics in the history of wheeled products: the 1983 creation of the brilliantly named H.O.G., the Harley Owner's Group. Within four years, 73,000 members were registered. Today, the number is almost half a million.

Today, if you buy a Harley, you receive a free one-year membership to H.O.G. with access to any of over nine hundred local chapters—the world's largest company-sponsored motorcycle enthusiast group. They conduct several national rallies and rallies in almost every state.

The group both reinforces each member's devotion to Harley and serves as Harley's most effective promotional vehicle. It also allows Harley executives to practice what the Japanese call *genchi genbutsu*: Go to the scene and learn what is happening, what you might call "marketing by walking around." Harley's executives and employees do this by attending H.O.G. events almost every weekend between Easter and Halloween, where they learn what bike owners love.

The authors of the H.O.G. website could have written a paragraph of this section, as you see in this excerpt:

> There's a basic human longing to be a part of something greater than yourself. We like to think of Harley-Davidson—from the top corporate officer to the newest Harley owner and rider—as one big, happy family....Does that sound like something you want to be a part of? Then join H.O.G. today.

H.O.G. illustrates a key trend: community as a service (CAAS). Good marketers always ask, "How can we bind our users together?" Nike does it by forming Nike running clubs at Nike stores nationwide.

Sony did it right inside its PlayStation, which uses the Internet to allow players all over the world to play together while they converse with each other over microphones and headsets.

Tazo promotes its teas as more than refreshments; they're a way to meet others. Tazo makes this clear with the printed messages on its store shelves: "Brew some tea. Enjoy good conversation. That's how friends are made."

American Express leverages CAAS, too. For years, it sold the security of its card—"Don't leave home without it"—and the card's prestige. Then the company decided it needed to sell a club instead and started calling its users "members," not "cardholders"; every American Express card says that.

In case we missed this point, American Express in 2007 decided to ensure that we wouldn't. No longer did it deliver messages like "Do you know me?" and "My life. My card," as it did in two very effective campaigns. It made sure people knew it was a club, not a card, by asking, "Are you a card *member*?"

But we save the biggest for last. In July 2010, when over 200 million people were playing online social games each month, Disney signaled its faith in an even bigger future by unloading $563 million to buy Playdom, a social game developer. The most popular of these online games are not one-on-one, but collaborative. It takes a village on phones and computers to play FarmVille, for example, where teams work together to raise barns and plow wheat fields. FarmVille's developer and the overwhelming leader in social game development, Zygna, signals its CAAS purpose in its motto: What could be clearer than its five words, "Connecting the world through games"?

Panera's Invisible Secret

"Why don't you eat at Ruggeri's anymore?"

That was a reasonable question to ask the former Ruggeri's waiter, because it often seemed that everyone in St. Louis was there, in the classic Italian restaurant in the heart of the city's Italian neighborhood, the Hill. The former waiter was Yogi Berra, who less than ten years later became famous as the catcher for the New York Yankees, and he responded to that question with an answer that became almost as famous as Yogi: "No one goes there anymore. It's too crowded."

To restaurateurs today, Yogi's days look like the good old ones. Tonight, you can walk into a restaurant where you once waited forty-five minutes to be seated and hear your request for a table echo off the walls.

But there's been one notable exception.

Despite a declining economy, Panera Bread's same-store sales increased 10.3 percent in the first quarter of 2010, after 3 percent increases in 2008 and 2009. Investors noticed; from 1999 to 2009, Panera was America's hottest restaurant stock, soaring 315 percent.

Panera builds off a strong concept—fast, healthy food—but few restaurants triumph from their food alone. McDonald's, for example, took over the world not because of its burgers but because in a world of "hamburger joints" and all that phrase implies—greasy spoons, old gum stuck under the tables, and restrooms few dared to enter—McDonald's burger restaurants were scrubbed spotless.

Panera's success rests on something beyond its speedy food, too.

If at almost any hour you peek through the intentionally large windows of your nearest Panera, you will notice lots of people. You assume they came for the food, and your confidence in the crowd draws you in. To enhance that feeling of welcome homeyness, every Panera is filled with a fragrance that has enchanted most of us since childhood: the smell of fresh-baked bread.

That aroma is one trick in cofounder Ron Shaich's bag of them that has made Panera thrive.

But there's one more: a truly invisible example of understanding our wish to be a part that almost everyone advised Shaich against.

In January 2005, Shaich began installing in Panera what is now the largest free WiFi network in the world. He was convinced that offering free WiFi would accomplish just what it has: turn his restaurants into gathering places. And how many people might Panera hope to gather there, at least now and then? Start with 22 million; that's the current number of officeless workers in America. For those 22 million, every Panera represents a possible office, complete with fresh coffee, warm smells, and the company of others.

Yes, Starbucks had the idea of being "America's third place," the place you went when you weren't in your other two places: your home and your office. But Starbucks, until it realized its mistake in June 2010, required you to buy a loyalty card and limited you to two hours of WiFi service. By charging nothing for unlimited service, Panera looks more like home; your mom and dad wouldn't charge you for Internet access, would they?

So Panera—coincidentally headquartered in Berra's and Ruggeri's hometown—seems to reverse Berra's famous quotation. People go to Panera because people go there, drawn partly by the day-long crowds they notice inside—and by the clever network they do not.

III. LOVERS OF THE FAMILIAR

———

At least once each year, a major American magazine decides to update its design to appear more current. Every time this happens, the magazine's editors brace themselves for what they know will follow: a flood of emails and letters from upset readers.

"Why fix what wasn't broken?" several subscribers will write. Whatever words they choose, these critics repeat one theme: We preferred the old look.

We keep seeing this; we strongly prefer the familiar, as the remarkable cases that follow suggest.

What *Was* in the Marshall Field's Name?

Within days after September 9, 2006, thousands of Chicagoans simply stopped going to the iconic Marshall Field's department store on State Street.

For years, that idea sounded unthinkable to native Chicagoans, because for most of its 125 years, Marshall Field's had served as Chicago's town square. Whenever two people visiting downtown wanted to meet, they usually followed the great Chicago tradition: "Let's meet under the clock at Marshall Field's."

In the fall of 2006, many stopped.

They weren't responding to a weak economy. That fall, America's economy reached fifth gear. It wasn't the store, either; it was the same store with the same merchandise—except one thing: the name.

Marshall Field's was now Macy's.

This was not the first time that Marshall Field's had stopped being the original Marshall Field's. Twenty-four years earlier, a British-based company, British and American Tobacco, had acquired it. Years later, Dayton Hudson of Minneapolis acquired it, which eventually led to Marshall Field's being owned and operated by Target. That changed yet again just years later, when Target sold Marshall Field's to the May Company.

Marshall Field's had not really been the classic Marshall Field's for decades. But until that fall and despite all those changes in ownership, Marshall Field's had continued to use the Marshall Field's name.

In changing the name to Macy's, it appeared to be swapping one iconic retailing name for an even bigger one. Macy's stores are immortalized in the movie *Miracle on 34th Street*, the site of midtown Manhattan's Macy's, and have been spectacularly branded into our American brains by Macy's famous annual Thanksgiving Day Parade, watched by an estimated 44 million viewers each year.

But when the change to the Macy's name was announced, crowds of protesters assembled—under the clock, of course—and gathered again to protest exactly one year later.

They wanted their Marshall Field's; they wanted that name and all that it evoked: shopping trips with best friends, Christmas displays and Christmas carols, Dad returning home with a Marshall Field's bag and a surprise inside. That the store was the same meant nothing; the *name* meant something. Without the name, the store was not the same— even though it was.

They wanted the familiar, and they wanted what Marshall Field's meant to them and had meant all their Chicagoland lives. They craved Marshall Field's the idea, and when the name was gone, that idea went with it.

We love the familiar, particularly one rich with meaning, and Marshall Field's meant presents, shopping, Christmas, and meeting best friends under the clock. We can tire of the familiar, but we never tire of great memories and the great brands that created them—as Macy's learned that day in September 2006.

The Fall, Rise, and Fall of *The Mary Tyler Moore Show*

From the beginning of television and for over twenty years after, the situation portrayed in every American situation comedy was the same, from *Father Knows Best* and *The Many Loves of Dobie Gillis* to *My Three Sons* and *The Adventures of Ozzie and Harriet*. Dads did not work, it appeared, but merely came home from work. When they opened the front door, they cried out, "Honey, I'm home!"

The adoring family rushed to meet the dad, and he tossed down his homburg hat, grabbed Mom around the waist of her just-pressed cotton dress, and said, "Hi, Little Rickie/Beaver/kids!"

Women were moms, usually in aprons, just coming from or returning to the kitchen. Moms and dads doted, never yelled, and offered wisdom. Sex had not been invented.

Fred MacMurray, the classic sitcom dad from *My Three Sons,* so illustrated this virginal perfection of parents that seeing *Double Indemnity* for the first time can be shocking. How could America's nicest dad possibly turn into Walter Neff? How could he smoke cigarettes and sneer, "Hey, baby"—*and to a married woman*? How could he covet that married barracuda Barbara Stanwyck and help murder her husband so that he and Black Widow could live happily ever after off the insurance settlement? That was television for over two decades: seventy different versions of *Father Knows Best But Doesn't Yell at, or Sleep with, Mom.*

Then came 1970.

Through most of 1969, James L. Brooks had been working on a pilot television show built around Rob Petrie's wife from *The Dick Van Dyke Show,* the actress Mary Tyler Moore. Because these were the years right after Woodstock, and of the pill, bra burning, *Ms.* magazine, and *Playboy,* Brooks envisioned a different sort of sitcom. The central woman wouldn't be a dutiful wife cooking all day but a single woman who pursued both a career and men.

Brooks also did not want to surround Mary with Ozzies, Beavers, and Wallys. Instead, he wanted people with edges and neuroses. So he created Ted Baxter, a pompous dimwit who believes himself the world's best broadcaster and a lady's man; Rhoda, Mary's loud, whiny, and promiscuous neighbor; and Lou, the gruff boss who yells.

Brooks's characters were people we could dislike, and test audiences did. *Intensely.*

The test audiences *hated* the show. We love smooth, and Rhoda wasn't. The audience members called her the opposite of smooth: "abrasive." Ted Baxter behaved too much like the employees too many of the testers knew from work: the inept narcissist and braggart.

They also loathed Phyllis, Mary's self-centered and self-important landlord, played perfectly by Cloris Leachman. Americans hate snobs, those who pretend not to know that all of us are created equal.

The audiences also struggled with Mary. She'd been married to that wonderful Rob Petrie for years, and now she was single and dating. How *could* she? Where was Rob?

The test audiences hated the show because it seemed so new and different. Like the songs on the CD we hate the first time, barely endure the second, and end up loving, our first exposure to something unfamiliar makes us uneasy, and we interpret unease like disease: something to be avoided.

The Mary Tyler Moore Show felt unfamiliar, and we love the familiar.

The tests nearly produced what now seems like a ridiculous result; *The Mary Tyler Moore Show* might never have aired. But by the time Brooks had finished this testing, it was too late for CBS to cancel the first airing. So episode one, "Love Is in the Air," ran.

Fortunately, people at home liked the show more than the testers had, but Brooks was still millions of watchers short of a hit. By season's end, the show gained some traction but still ranked only twenty-second of all shows on television.

The show rolled into year two, and roll it did. It shot up to tenth in the 1971–1972 season, then up again to seventh in 1972–1973. It was a hit, en route to becoming a legend, the program often called the best comedy in television history.

What happened? Why did Mary fail in testing and thrive on television?

It's because the unfamiliar became familiar.

Like the song on the CD that finally gets us singing along on the fourth listening, people finally got comfortable with Ted, Phyllis, Rhoda, and Mary. Americans liked that these people were like each of us: flawed. Lou raged, Ted connived, Phyllis preened, Rhoda pouted. It was a show where fathers didn't know best; Ted Baxter didn't know anything. *That* seemed familiar.

Then what happened?

Over the next two years, Mary's show slipped slightly, ranking ninth and then eleventh. And then came 1975–1976.

In that season, the show dropped to number nineteen: a warning flare. In 1976–1977, it plummeted to thirty-ninth, and on March 19, 1977, in perhaps one of the most memorable endings to any TV show ever, Mary walked out of the WJM newsroom and turned out the lights. Screens across America went black for several seconds.

Then that door creaked open. Mary peeked back into the room, then closed the door again for the last time.

Why did *Mary*'s star burn so bright yet fall so fast? *It's because the familiar always becomes too familiar. Mary*'s writers ran out of new twists and characters. The addition of Betty White as Sue Ann Nivens, the "Happy Homemaker" and television's first cougar, helped in 1974, and adding sweet but clueless Georgette two years earlier may have, too. Ultimately, however, new always gets old.

To complicate *Mary*'s problem, what had made the show so unfamiliar at first—its abrasive characters—worked so well that every network started casting abrasives. A season after *Mary* appeared, NBC gave us perhaps the most abrasive character in television history: Archie Bunker of *All in the Family,* which became America's most-watched program in *Mary*'s second season.

Wow! Producers decided, if this gruff, homophobic, racist, flag-waving and hippie-hating Archie could work, why not an abrasive black man who seemed to hate *everyone* and every thing, a man who in the spirit of the Me Century was a classic narcissist? Thus was born George Jefferson of *The Jeffersons,* which reached number four in *Mary*'s fifth season. George and his family might have climbed even higher in the ratings had it not been for a competing abrasive black man: Sanford, played by Redd Foxx on *Sanford and Son.* That show ranked second that year.

Two producers in Los Angeles then made an obvious choice. If two insufferable black men and an insufferable right-wing male bigot could work, what about creating a program featuring an insufferable and abrasive *liberal woman*?

Voilà! The world flocked to watch Bea Arthur in *Maude,* the ninth-most-watched show of that same year.

What about Mary's "abrasive" friend Rhoda and her egomaniacal landlady Phyllis, whom *The Mary Tyler Moore Show* testers hated? Well, of course: They got their own shows. The next year, *Phyllis* ranked sixth, *Rhoda* finished ninth.

You can guess what happened next.

The familiar became tedious. A year later, *Phyllis* and *Rhoda* dove out of the top twenty. The networks canceled *Phyllis* at the end of the season and *Rhoda* at the end of the next.

If anyone wonders why car makers change cars every year and software companies introduce new versions within what seems like eight weeks of the previous release; if people wonder why Madonna keeps morphing into new versions that barely resemble her previous one, just as Christina Aguilera does; or why *Monday Night Football* introduces new stars, new music, new promos every season, despite their enormous cost; if anyone wonders about any of these phenomena and many others, the history of the 1970s sitcom provides the answer:

We want the familiar. Until it becomes too familiar.

How the Mop Tops Cleaned Up

On February 9, 1964, minutes after 8 p.m. eastern time, America's crime rate dropped dramatically for twenty minutes, and the American barbering industry fell into a recession that would last almost twenty years.

That was the night the Beatles first appeared on American television, on CBS's *The Ed Sullivan Show*, and launched America into Beatlemania. Over 73 million Americans watched, an astonishing one of every three American men, women, and children. Our streets were empty.

Now, more than forty years later, we assume that the four fellows' talent made it inevitable that *Rolling Stone* one day would name them the number-one singing group of all time and that *Time* magazine would name them among the 100 Most Influential People of the Century. But the four Brits' triumph, it turns out, involved something more. It involved a fifth Brit, one with a clever insight into Americans and a pioneer in the art of what today is a marketing mantra, "engaging the customer."

We begin with a fact that will shock many people: The Beatles initially appeared doomed in America. Just months after they emerged as a phenomenon in their native England, EMI offered Capitol Records the rights to release the group's single "Please Please Me" in the United States; Capitol refused. EMI then turned to Atlantic Records and offered it the same opportunity.

Atlantic refused, too.

Finally, EMI convinced a small label called Vee-Jay to take on the single, which it eventually released on February 7, 1963—what turned out to be a year to the day before the Beatles landed in America for the first time. But their single didn't please Americans at all; it sold only 7,310 copies.

The failure of "Please Please Me" seemed to prove that the executives at Capitol and Atlantic had been right for passing on the Beatles and for recognizing a pattern in American music. On the date of the single's release, only one British act had ever reached the American top ten: Frankie Ifield's "I Remember You," which turned out to be Ifield's only American hit. American record executives decided there was a law at work: British acts don't work here.

On September 28, these executives looked astute. That was the night that the era's most famous disc jockey, Murray the K, played the Beatles' "She Loves You" on New York's monster rock and roll station, 1010 WINS. If any DJ could make a record move in those days, it was Murray the K. But no one seemed to be listening that night; Murray's phones went silent.

A month later, those executives looked even more astute. That was the October afternoon that Dick Clark debuted "She Loves You" on the Rate-A-Record segment of his popular Saturday-afternoon rock and roll show, *American Bandstand*.

Clark's teenage panelists gave the song a barely

passing grade: 71 of a possible 98 points. That wasn't the worst news for the boys, however. When Clark showed a photo of the foursome to some audience members, they laughed. They giggled over the Beatles' haircuts, which quickly earned the name "mop tops" because they looked like mops on the fellows' heads. And it didn't help that the four Brits wore collarless jackets and high-heeled Italian leather boots with long pointed toes, wardrobe choices that in 1963 would have gotten them rolled in half of America's bars.

Clark had aired the song only as a favor. His friend Bernie Binnick had acquired the song's American rights earlier that summer and, knowing the impact of a *Bandstand* appearance, approached Clark. Binnick insisted that the Beatles' mix of the familiar—an American sound that was part Buddy Holly, part Chuck Berry—and the new—their "mod" look—could combine to produce a hit.

Clark's reply would be historic: "You're absolutely insane. It'll never fly."

"Please Please Me" had failed; Capital and Atlantic had passed. "She Loves You" had failed; Clark's audience had laughed, and Clark was recommending therapy for anyone who thought the Beatles could succeed. The song never reached the *Billboard* charts.

Worried but undeterred, a fifth man went to

work: Brian Epstein, the band's manager. On November 5, the day after the group's command performance before the British royal family, he flew to New York on a trip he had planned to promote another British singer, Billy J. Kramer. Just days before, Epstein's friend and Ed Sullivan's European talent coordinator, Peter Prichard, called Epstein. Having recently seen the Beatles perform, Prichard encouraged Epstein to coax Sullivan to host the Beatles on his show. While Epstein was en route to New York, Prichard called Sullivan and told him of the group's command performance, impressing Sullivan with the fact that the Beatles were the first "long-haired boys" ever invited to appear before the queen of England.

Here, too, luck intervened.

Just twelve days earlier, Sullivan and his wife Sylvia had been delayed at London's Heathrow Airport. Looking through a pouring rain outside, Sullivan and Sylvia could not miss the spectacle: over 1,500 anxious and sopping-wet young Brits lining the rooftop of the Queen's Building and the grounds. For what? Sullivan asked a passerby, and learned they were there to see the Beatles.

"Who the hell are they?" he asked.

"A huge pop group here. Returning from a tour of Sweden."

Sullivan's immediate thought: Elvis Presley. Only Elvis had ever inspired a mania like the one that he and Sylvia were seeing outside that Heathrow Airport window. So when Epstein approached him about the Beatles twelve days later, Sullivan was primed.

Ultimately the two agreed to a contract that few people can hear about today without gasping. For three performances, the foursome and Epstein would divide up $10,000, just over $650 per person per appearance. Perhaps sensing he'd done too well in the negotiations, Sullivan agreed to throw in the group's transportation and lodging.

The Sullivan deal opened the American pipeline from England. When Capitol Records executives learned about it, they recognized that the exposure on Sullivan's show would produce record sales that at least covered their costs and finally signed a deal with Epstein.

But Epstein still agonized.

The Dick Clark and Murray the K experiences troubled him. He had difficulty disregarding the views of Clark, who was America's leading taste-maker and talent spotter in rock and roll. Epstein reasonably feared that the Beatles would not be accepted; they were too unfamiliar, too odd-looking, too feminine.

So Epstein set to work.

Fearing that the Beatles would look too unfamiliar to American audiences, he decided he had to make us feel comfortable with them and to welcome to America what soon would be called "The British Invasion." To complicate his task, however, these working lads from Liverpool had spent their formative years playing in Hamburg's red-light district, and they did not always wear well.

John was prickly and abrasive; Ringo fidgeted in front of cameras and microphones, had a face made for radio, and looked awkward (playing a right-handed drum set left handed may have added to Ringo's apparent problem). George's face exuded bottomless vacancy and detachment. Paul looked cute, but so did Natalie Wood, to whom he bore too close a resemblance for some American men.

So for the album that would break the ice in America, to be released twenty days before the first Sullivan appearance, Epstein ignored the common practice of naming the album after the title of its biggest hit. Instead, Epstein wanted to make a connection between his alien band and the American audience. So he gave the album a title that invited us to become friends of his foreign invaders. He called it *Meet the Beatles!*

Epstein was inviting us in. If we doubt this ploy, we should go online and read the playlist on the album's back cover: "I Want to Hold *Your* Hand." "Till There Was *You*." "I Wanna Be *Your* Man." His boys were talking to each of us.

Now look at the very first lyrics of some of the songs on the album:

"Close your eyes and I'll kiss *you*"

"It won't be long, yeh, yeh, yeh... 'til I belong to *you*."

"Whenever I want *you* around..."

"Little child, little child, won't *you* dance with me?"

"You know *you* made me cry..."

Meet the Beatles! invited us to meet them, to be a part of them. Having invited *you* in on its cover, the Beatles did not sing about Maybelline or Run-around Sue. They sang about each of us, soon to be the centerpieces of the Me Decade. The Beatles serenaded us, just as advertising copywriters do when they repeatedly use the word "you" in ads and commercials, even though they are writing to everyone. The songs on *Meet the Beatles!* are not just songs but conversations with us set to 4/4 time, Paul's German guitar, and Ringo's black Ludwig drums.

To make sure the boys connected with the Americans, Epstein stage-managed Sullivan's brief interviews with the foursome: Be upbeat, he insisted, be one of them. ("John, be sweet for six seconds.") Epstein understood our wish to feel a part, our discomfort with the unfamiliar, and our dislike of those who "put on airs." Like many Brits, he also understood both our optimism and our unusual need for a major dose of it that night in February. Just seventy-eight days earlier, we had suffered one of the great traumas of our century: the assassination of President Kennedy.

Fortunately for Epstein, the boys were at their upbeat best—so much so that at the conclusion of their third and final appearance, on February 23, Sullivan thanked them, memorably referring to them as "four of the nicest youngsters."

Today, few people question the group's claim to be history's greatest recording group. But Epstein knew what we loved; like children, we are self-centered. We want even our songs to be about us and our entertainers to talk to us.

Epstein got us, and that helped the Beatles make history. The following August, they were movie stars, too, with the U.S. release of *A Hard Day's Night*, which *Time* magazine years later named one of the one hundred greatest movies of all time. (Remarkably, Dick Clark still wasn't convinced. He told a *Philadelphia Inquirer* reporter, "Beatlemania is fading. Their music is kid stuff.")

Once Epstein made the Fab Four familiar to us, he refused to let them become too familiar. From the sweet and innocent rock of *Meet the*

Beatles!, Epstein and Lennon-McCartney shifted gears, releasing their folk-rockish *Rubber Soul* just two years later.

Less than a year after that, they released their guitar-driven *Revolver,* followed by their masterpiece, the psychedelic-rock *Sgt. Pepper's Lonely Hearts Club Band,* famously packaged to suggest that the band included heavyweight boxer Sonny Liston, Marilyn Monroe, W. C. Fields, Bob Dylan, and a particular band favorite, Marlon Brando. The Lonely Hearts Club Band was one of us, the all-American band, the album cover told us.

And wouldn't you know, the boys had learned that we needed to feel familiar with this new group, too, just as we had back in 1964. Within seconds of *Sgt. Pepper's* first chord, they ask us,

> *So may I introduce to* you
> *The act* you've *known for all these years,*
> *Sergeant Pepper's Lonely Hearts Club Band.*

See what they just said again? We're new, but we're familiar. You've known us all this time; meet us once again.

After they first heard the song on July 25, 1965, music legends Carole King and Frank Zappa separately told friends they were considering quitting music. Across the country in Seattle at the same time, another legend heard the song on the radio and reached a slightly different decision: Jimi Hendrix told himself he was still a guitarist but no longer a singer.

The wonder was that these three legends ever heard the song "Like a Rolling Stone" at all.

Five weeks earlier, Columbia Records' marketing executives first heard the song and, like Dick Clark hearing the Beatles, insisted the song would never fly. It was 6:09 long, and only two six-minute songs had ever reached the *Billboard* Top 100. The song was an unfamiliar fusion: folk-music lyrics, electronic rock guitars, and classic piano and organ. The organist himself was a twenty-one-year-old session guitarist named Al Kooper who had never played the organ before, and it showed: He played an eighth-note behind the other instruments.

The song might never have been released had it not been for two Dylan fans at Columbia Records. They snuck copies of the track to Terry Noel, America's first celebrity deejay, who was working Manhattan's hottest disco, Arthur. Noel liked it, played it, and reported back that his celebrity audience did, too.

But even after hearing this, Columbia's executives still feared the song would never fly, that the celebrities at Arthur were chasms apart from the typical

American record buyer. But they finally caved and on July 20 released "Like a Rolling Stone."

Within days it reached *Billboard*'s number two. It stayed in the top ten for sixteen weeks, an impressive tenure then and now. Forty years later, the British rock magazine *Mojo* named it the greatest single in rock music history, an honor bestowed on it by *Rolling Stone* a year later.

Like Dick Clark contemplating the Beatles and CBS executives considering the pilot for *The Mary Tyler Moore Show*, Columbia's executives' handling of Dylan's song reminds us how inexpert expert opinion can be. As important, it underscores how quickly we reject the unfamiliar. Six minutes of dense and not always comprehensible metaphors ("Napoleon in rags, and the language that he used"), an off-beat organ, a folk singer with a gravelly voice playing an electric guitar—it sounded like nothing they'd heard before.

It was a classic human error: concluding too much from too little. Six-minute songs routinely failed, but then studios had decided that quickly and stopped releasing those songs. So the executives' sample of long songs was too small. Their bigger error, however, was that Columbia's thirty-five-year-old executives thought they knew what twenty-year-olds loved. But in the 1960s, the answer to the question "What do kids love?" was

"Whatever adults don't." A catchphrase of 1960s youth captures this perfectly: "Never trust anyone over thirty."

Incomprehensible lyrics? If anything, that was the appeal of the classic "Louie Louie" just years before and of Nirvana's classic "Smells Like Teen Spirit" many years later.

The executives also failed to realize that after a week at a beach, you stop noticing the ocean's roar at night. The radio plays a song several times, and with each playing the listener adapts: the unfamiliar becomes just familiar enough. And sometimes, like *Mary Tyler Moore, 60 Minutes*, the Beatles, and the greatest song in rock history, the unfamiliar becomes a classic.

A Sunday with Christina Applegate

Just before 11 a.m. on a Sunday morning in February 2000, we are driving south in Beverly Hills en route to a celebrated church.

My friend has breathlessly told me three times that the church's leader is renowned in New Age circles, a circle which, from my visits to her San Diego church, seemed to have as its first commandment "Whatever Works." (Because her church seemed so forgiving that it had banished the very idea of sin, I had started calling it "The Church of the Holy Go-For-It.")

Two blocks from the church, the backed-up traffic signaled that my companion was right: The New Age was descending on this Beverly Hills church. We finally found a vacant parking spot far from the entrance, made the trek, and found an eighth-row seat.

Seconds later, two women sat down in the two aisle seats on our right.

Over the next seventy-five minutes, I glanced at these women several times. I wasn't drawn by their faces but by the palpable warmth between them, and I deduced they were mother and daughter. Nothing else about them caught my attention.

After the ceremony, my friend and I inched from our seats into the 1,100 people squeezing out the doors. I noticed that fair-haired mother and daughter immediately in front of us.

Halfway to the door, my companion leaned in toward me.

"Do you recognize *her*?" she whispered in a tone that suggested I should.

"Should I?" I replied.

"Oh, yes! That's Christina Applegate. The TV star. *Married with Children*."

"She's a TV star? *Her*?" I said.

I responded that way because in real life, or at least on that Sunday of my real life, Christina Applegate looked like a girl we might run into on almost any block of Ames, Iowa, or Spokane, Washington. Christina Applegate, by all accounts, is a pretty woman. And like almost every pretty woman, her face displays one signal trait: *It is remarkably average.*

Christina Applegate has an average nose; it's not big, it's not little. Her eyes are a fraction bigger than average, and her eyes look slightly grayer than the average brown eyes. She has nice skin, a shade lighter than average, certainly not more luminous than average. With the help of Hollywood makeup artists, Applegate's generally average features become very attractive to most people.

Interestingly, we also find most attractive the things that look familiar—including faces. (Not surprising, considering that in our distant past, an unfamiliar face could belong to an enemy or intruder.) We like eyes that are the average distance apart and average-size noses that are the average distance from the top and bottom lips. Cameron Diaz, as one useful example, possesses an almost perfectly symmetrical face, an average nose, attractive but not unusual eyes, attractive but not memorable hair, a light but familiar tone of skin. Interestingly, most people do not describe Diaz as uniquely attractive, almost certainly because of her one far-from-average feature: her mouth. It seems to begin at her left ear and end at her right.

We are more tolerant of a larger-than-average mouth, however, because it facilitates something else Cameron Diaz has: an enormous smile that makes the Cheshire Cat look gloomy by comparison. Smiles comfort us; they signal, "I am a blessing, not a danger," and they radiate optimism, something to which we are uniquely attracted.

At this point at least one reader has rebelled, having had a sudden vision of one startling beauty: the actress Penelope Cruz. Cruz has unusually dark skin, unusually large and seemingly black eyes, almost black hair, and a much longer than average nose with an unusually prominent tip that is very close to her top lip. Nothing is average, and Cruz looks dazzling.

But are we truly and totally attracted to faces like hers? Woody Allen, who directed Cruz's Oscar-winning performance in *Vicky Cristina Barcelona*, told a *Vanity Fair* reporter something that echoes what many people feel in Cruz's presence: uncomfortable.

"I cannot take her face in all at once," Allen said. "It's too overwhelming."

Just days after I first wrote this, I walked to check out some apple fritters from my Lunds grocery stores and was stopped cold. Right in front of the checkout I spied the cover of the new issue of *People* and its annual announcement of the Most Beautiful Person in the World. Their choice? *Christina Applegate.*

Why? It's because she's a perfect combination of remarkably average features, and a face filled with average features, the most familiar ones, looks beautiful to us. Her face is simple, smooth, easy on the eyes—a collection of average features, symmetrically assembled on a face we might see one day in Ames or Spokane.

This preference of ours for the average and familiar is so strong and common that scholars have given it a name: koinophilia. That word derives from the Greek *koinos,* which means "usual," and *philos*, which means "love," so koinophilia literally means "love of the usual."

Might this explain the enthuasism over Apple's 2010 introduction of Flipboard? The genius of Flipboard is that it takes a person's collections of their friends' Facebook and Twitter updates and turns them into something very familiar looking: a magazine.

So it is true in our preferences for beauty, too: We love the familiar.

How the New Gets Old: The Ocean That Stopped Roaring

On the evening of Friday, January 26, 1968, Jeff Greendorfer and his college roommate arrived at his roommate's home on a cliff on the northern Oregon Coast. It was Jeff's first visit to Oregon's coast, but he knew the Pacific Ocean well, having grown up minutes from it in San Francisco. To give Jeff the full benefit of his visit, his hosts assigned him the green bedroom, from which he was able to look out its floor-to-ceiling window and see thirty miles out to sea.

That night was Jeff's last in the room.

The next morning at breakfast, Jeff apologized to three hosts. He felt grateful for being given the room with the best view in the house but couldn't sleep there again. "The waves sound so loud, they kind of scare me."

Jeff's announcement startled his hosts. They'd lived alongside the ocean for decades, so the ocean sounded different to them; it did not sound at all.

Jeff's hosts had experienced what psychologists call perceptual adaptation: they'd adapted to what they heard to the point where they no longer heard it. That is why advertisers change ads often. We become so accustomed to ads that we cease to notice them, just like Jeff's hosts no longer noticed the crash of the waves on the rocks below.

Familiarity breeds numbness. This is why we often struggle with marriage. Each partner becomes habituated; we notice less, which causes us to appreciate less. This also explains why receiving a gift at an unexpected time makes us smile for several days, but a birthday gift—being expected—usually touches us less.

We love what is familiar, and then we don't.

Familiarity eventually breeds fatigue, but until that occurs, we crave what is familiar and recoil at what is not, as Mary Tyler Moore discovered in the middle of the 1970s.

And it's the tightrope several American companies are now walking.

It is August 9, 2009. The wires release a report from Howard Schultz in Seattle: Starbucks is closing three hundred stores and laying off workers. Experienced readers of these cutback press releases brace for what they know will come next: the addendum "We believe these changes will prepare us for the success we project as economic conditions improve."

Commentators quickly pointed to an explanation for Starbucks' struggles: McDonald's. McDonald's had invested multimillions in promoting its McCafé, so surely its gain explained Starbucks' loss. Or was Starbucks simply experiencing what Mary, Rhoda, and Phyllis experienced? One day you seem fresh, and the next day you taste stale.

Starbucks may be reenacting the Gap saga. That's where one day you are the store everyone drives blocks for, the next day you are the store on every block, and the day after that you are on the block for sale, for anyone willing to buy something that has become too familiar.

Gap, however, looks vibrant to the people working at Home Office, 6301 Fitch Path, in New Albany, Ohio, today.

That's the campus office headquarters of Abercrombie & Fitch, whose sales in June 2009 free-fell an alarming 28 percent. It is too early to predict the *Mary Tyler Moore* fate for the retailer, and it's risky, because A&F has proven its special insight into its tightly defined, eighteen-to-twenty-two-year-old market. Its design and concept are brilliant enough. Among other benefits, its 90-decibel electronic dance music discourages anyone over forty from entering an A&F, as does that scent wafting through every row; it's A&F's own Fierce, a phenomenal fragrance that shouts teenage hormones.

A&F also smartly diversified. It introduced Hollister to combat A&F brand fatigue and Gilly Hicks to trade on the company's sexualized image by moving into women's underwear and loungewear. But the risks to the core Abercrombie & Fitch brand are there; its challenge is to be just fresh enough, to be familiar without being too familiar.

That's the challenge of every marketer today: How do we avoid becoming *Mary Tyler Moore*— old news just months after being America's favorite show?

GM and Ford: Did Their Familiarity Breed Our Contempt?

In 1958, a physician practicing in Wheeler, Oregon, on the northern Oregon coast splurged on a new car to replace his beloved 1949 Packard. It was a beige 1958 Mercedes-Benz 190, with its signature red leather upholstery and wooden window frames and door trim. No one in tiny Tillamook County had ever seen a Mercedes. Almost every day some-one asked him, "Just what kinda car is that?"

Fourteen years later, his son, living in what soon would be called the Silicon Valley, bought a 1972 BMW 2002. Despite the affluence of that area south of San Francisco, BMWs were so uncommon in 1972 that BMW owners comprised a cult, com-plete with a club signal. Every time a BMW owner spotted another BMW approaching, he would flash his headlights on and off.

Today, BMW and Mercedes, along with their fellow German carmakers Porsche and Audi, dominate the higher end of the American car market, while the Japanese, comparatively recent arrivals in our country, threaten to dominate the lower and middle, and together, they help explain the problems of Ford and General Motors, which came to a head when our economy nearly collapsed in 2008.

But as you consider that many imports are relatively new to this country, and Ford and Chevrolet are so relatively old, it seems worth asking: Is that part of the problem of America's car manufacturers? Have American cars become like Gap stores and Krispy Kremes, just too common and too familiar?

Toyota must think so; it must sense how easily we tire of the familiar. When Toyota decided to grab more of the high and low ends of the car markets, it created Lexus and Scion.

The first breakout Japanese brand, Datsun, which captivated American car buyers with its iconic 240Z in 1972, abandoned the Datsun name in 1981 for a new one, Nissan. Then, as Japanese and German cars began to become almost too familiar to us, that created an opening for another new brand. Cooper seized that opportunity with its unconventional Mini Cooper and equally unconventional advertising.

We love the familiar, but then it becomes too familiar. We are known for tiring of the old.

We regularly destroy our great old buildings, as one sad example. The two great buildings of the beginning of the last century in Minneapolis—the West Hotel and the fabulous Metropolitan Building, which *Harper's* once featured on its cover—were demolished less than forty years after they were built. Sociologists routinely observe that people of most countries venerate their old, look to them for wisdom, and live under the same roofs, but Americans discard their old. Our work policies treat men and women over sixty-four as apparent liabilities and wrinkled skin as a fate to be avoided at billions in annual costs.

Are Ford and Chevrolet poorly managed and hopelessly handicapped by their health care and labor costs? Perhaps. But these companies could solve those problems and still have this one: *They are old and too familiar.* To thrive, Ford and GM may have to become new again, or we will continue to treat them as we treat our aging buildings and aging people: Out with the old and too familiar, and in with the new.

The opportunity is there; the Fords of this world have an enormous advantage that appears to be growing with every decade: the unique power and influence of brands. Brands derive their power from the Rule of Familiarity. Brands are familiar and proven to us, which reassures us. Genuine innovations, by contrast, are neither familiar nor proven, which makes us uneasy. But when a branded company like Ford introduces an innovative product, its brand makes the product both familiar and new—intriguing and reassuring to us at the same time. So whatever else we come across in our road ahead, we will see brands in the drivers' seats.

Our era's most successful investor agrees. Look at Warren Buffett's seven largest holdings: Coca-Cola (almost 20 percent of his portfolio), Wells Fargo, Burlington Northern Santa Fe, Procter & Gamble, American Express, Kraft Foods, and Wal-Mart: a brand hall of fame. With that fame has come wealth; over the last ten years, Buffett's stocks have outperformed the market average by over 7 percent annually, a signal that brands are only increasing their unique influence over the products and services that we choose—and even the investments that we make.

IV. Eternal Optimists

—

Hello, Norma Jeane

A dutiful reader will email us soon with the answer to this trivia question: What television character, when asked about how she wanted to be treated after she died, answered, "I want you to take my ashes and spread them all over Burt Reynolds"?

Her idea seemed comical at the time. But not long after, life imitated television.

The bizarre tale begins after the wedding of the famous baseball player Joe DiMaggio and the actress Marilyn Monroe. During the marriage, the dutiful DiMaggio learned that Marilyn had bought a crypt at Pierce Brothers Westwood Village Memorial Park in Los Angeles. So he decided to purchase two himself: one directly above hers, the other adjacent.

When the couple divorced in 1954, DiMaggio chose to divorce her in death, too, and sold the crypt above hers to a friend, Richard Posner.

Eight years later, Monroe died.

We flash forward to 1986. Posner became ill. Sensing he was dying, he summoned his wife, Elsie, close to him as he lay in bed. "Lean down," he said, and she did. And then he whispered to her, "If I croak, if you don't put me upside down over Marilyn, I'll haunt you the rest of your life."

Apparently dutiful herself, Elsie Posner later obliged her husband's last request. "I was standing right there," she later told a *Los Angeles Times* reporter, "and the funeral director turned him over."

Now we flash forward to 2009. Feeling the weight of a $1.8 million mortgage on her Beverly Hills home and wanting to pass the home to her children without any encumbrances, Elsie got a thoroughly modern idea: She would auction off the crypt on eBay.

She set a starting price of $500,000. But when the bidding frenzy ended in late August, Elsie Posner had another enormous reason to bless the memory of her ex-husband Richard. The crypt he had bought from DiMaggio went for $4.6 million.

This short story perfectly captures us. It reveals the spread of technology with the eBay auction; our fascination with celebrity and their deaths; our affluence that leaves some of us with $4 million to spend on a hole in a wall; and our fascination with sex.

Religion works its way in here, too, obviously. Mr. Posner believed in life after death, like most Americans. We believe to an extent unmatched almost anywhere. According to a recent Pew report, 82 percent of us believe in God, and 9 percent believe in some other higher power; 74 percent believe in life after death, and 85 percent believe in heaven (although one in three Protestants believes that only Christians gain admittance there). Only one in twenty-five of us claims to be atheist or agnostic.

Clearly, Richard Posner believed. But his belief went beyond that and demonstrated one of our most remarked-upon traits: our bigger-than-Texas optimism. Richard Posner obviously did not believe just in life after death; he believed in sex after death, too. And his only-in-America optimism led him to believe not just in sex after death but in sex with the sex symbol of his entire generation, through four feet of concrete, in a memorial park in Los Angeles, California.

Welcome to America the Optimistic.

On March 24, 2005, Americans witnessed a new import from England: a television show. It was called *The Office,* and a year later it won an Emmy as television's outstanding comedy series.

The original version of the program aired in the United Kingdom in 2001 and was created by Stephen Merchant and the comedian Richard Gervais. America was not the first country to receive an imported version; the French adaptation *Le Bureau* aired in 2004.

When Gervais began to create the American version, however, he realized it would have to be different, because we are. When later asked about this, he noted four major differences between Americans and Brits: "You're smarter, you have better teeth, you're more ambitious, you're slightly broader." Then the comedian turned more serious, to a fifth difference: "But the big difference, Americans are more optimistic. You are told you can be the next president of the United States, and you can. In Britain, it's 'What happened to you?' "

Gervais knew about American optimism because he'd seen American movies, which for forty years had ended the way you'd expect in a nation of optimists: happily. They're so predictable that when the screenwriter in Robert Altman's satire of American moviemaking, *The Player,* insists that he's not going for a happy ending, he observes, "It's not even an American film at all."

In 1969, Gervais was only eight years old, so

he missed a rare period of Hollywood films that might have led him to view us differently. All four of that year's top-grossing films—*Butch Cassidy and the Sundance Kid, They Shoot Horses, Don't They?, Midnight Cowboy,* and *Easy Rider*—ended unhappily. Butch and Sundance, *Cowboy*'s Ratzo Rizzo, and *Easy Rider*'s Wyatt and Billy all die, and *Horses*' Jane Fonda character is arrested for her mercy killing of a marathon dancer.

What accounts for this unusual year in American film? Consider our culture in the few years leading up to it: the assassination of John F. Kennedy (1963), Martin Luther King, Jr., (1968), and Robert Kennedy (1969), and the escalation of both the war in Vietnam and the American protests against it. Is it surprising, then, that both the happy ending and the American comedy suffered from 1969 to 1971, and that among the very few top-grossing comedies we had *M*A*S*H** and *Catch-22,* which were a genre all to themselves—the antiwar comedy, with tones more cynical than comical?

But that was then. Of course, today we occasionally see sad endings—*Terms of Endearment* in 1983 and *Steel Magnolias* in 1989, for example. But they're the exceptions that prove the rule: Americans believe in happy endings. But then, what else would optimists believe in?

*   *   *

We believe.

We buy thousands of copies of "believe" songs from Mac Davis, Brooks & Dunn, and the Platters. If it rains today, we know tomorrow will be a brand-new day; this optimism features in the titles of songs by Sting, Michael Jackson, and Van Morrison, and in the musical about *The Wizard of Oz, The Wiz,* and echoes in the musical about Little Orphan Annie, *Annie*: "The sun will come out tomorrow, bet your bottom dollar."

In America, even our orphans believe everything will come out okay.

We believe in optimism and insist that others share it. You see it in our politics, on a bumper sticker that started appearing in 2009: "Annoy a liberal. Work hard and *be happy.*" That sentiment suggests that conservatives do not merely disagree with liberals' politics; they disagree with their negative attitudes. Liberals always are unhappy: wars in the Middle East, income equality, the condition of the economy. Don't worry, liberals, the bumper sticker urges them. Be happy.

We see this everywhere we look. Indeed, while we might worry about the apparent increases in narcissistic behavior, we also might consider this: Narcissists are likely to call themselves very attractive and are very likely to make $70,000 a year by the time they reach age thirty. But wouldn't optimists do that, too—and isn't optimism one of our most valuable traits?

That's the conclusion of the professor David Landes. In his exhaustive look at world economic history, *The Wealth and Poverty of Nations,* he concludes that optimism is the salient trait of great nations.

> In this world, the optimists have it, not because they are always right, but because they are positive....[T]hat is the way of achievement, civilization, achievement and success.... Educated, eye-open optimism pays.

And we certainly have it. In a December 2008 Harris Interactive/*Financial Times* survey, majorities in France (63 percent), Italy (62 percent), Spain (59 percent), Great Britain (58 percent), and Germany (52 percent) were pessimistic about their own economic situation. But 54 percent of Americans were optimistic about theirs. In a separate question, 83 percent of the French, 74 percent of Italians, 70 percent of Brits and Spaniards, and 63 percent of Germans said they were pessimistic about their country's economic status. And the Americans? Only 52 percent of us felt pessimistic.

Harris regularly asks Americans about our overall

life satisfaction. In October of 2009, 65 percent of us reported being very satisfied with the life we lead. In a Europe–U.S. comparison survey a few years earlier, 58 percent of Americans were very satisfied, almost twice the percentage found in Europe.

Even when our economy looked worse, in the middle of 2009, we held strong. In an ABC News/*Washington Post* poll, 75 percent of those surveyed had experienced the job or pay cut of a close friend or family member, yet two-thirds said they felt optimistic about their own family's future in the next twelve months, a percentage about the same as researchers had found the year before.

Two final telling statistics reflect our cheery outlook. A recent study found that over 80 percent of us believe in miracles. While this doesn't surprise American readers, it just startled the readers of this book's German and French translations; only 39 percent of Germans and 37 percent of French people believe in miracles. What they are most likely to believe in instead is that their day has passed.

We believe in miracles on earth and miracles after it. Again, over 80 percent of us believe in life after death, but only half of French people do. This is not surprising, given that the classic French work of literature *Candide* (its full French title is *Candide, ou l'Optimisme*) is a merciless attack on the optimism of the philosopher Gottfried Leibniz and is the book that brought the word "optimism" into our language, just after the American Revolution.

Perhaps this most clearly reveals just how new optimism is; the word itself is only, and exactly, three hundred years old as this is being printed.

Where did we get all this cheeriness and confidence? Might our history explain it?

Our ancestors arrived with all of their clothes on their backs or in tiny bags, many with valuable stamps or coins that they could exchange for a few months' food and rent, and within decades they built an empire of mills and factories and all their products, turning our unique abundance into even more abundance. The historian David Potter thought this was the case, considering our character so much a product of our abundance that he titled his classic work on the American character *People of Plenty*.

We became the planet's great believers, almost all of us to some degree a Jay Gatsby. By the end of Fitzgerald's great American novel *The Great Gatsby*, we learn that this man with a closetful of Egyptian cotton shirts of every color and a sprawling estate overlooking Long Island Sound is actually Jimmy Gatz, the son of a poor Minnesota farmer. We learn he had risen each day at 6 a.m., exercised from 6:15 to 6:30, studied from 7:15 to 8:15, worked for eight hours, and from 5 until 9 p.m. practiced "elocution, poise and how to attain it."

When Americans returned from World War II, millions of them made *South Pacific* among the most successful musicals, and later movies, of all time. Its music—two songs particularly—seem to perfectly capture American optimism. One song sounds like *The Power of Positive Thinking.* It's "Happy Talk":

> Happy talk, keep talkin' happy talk,
> Talk about things you'd like to do.
> You gotta have a dream.
> If you don't have a dream,
> How you gonna have a dream come true?

Lest we were in doubt about the relentless hopefulness of this musical, set during a war of all settings, another hit from the show makes the message even clearer:

> I could say life is just a bowl of Jell-O
> And appear more intelligent and smart,
> But I'm stuck like a dope
> With a thing called hope,
> And I can't get it out of my heart!

The song was called "A Cockeyed Optimist," and our cockeyed optimism only grew from there. We

saw two Kennedys and Martin Luther King assas-
sinated, an Asian war drag on without resolution,
a president impeached, the Twin Towers collapse,
and a deepening financial recession. Yet after all
that, two years after the Towers fell, Ricky Gervais
looked hard at us, took the American pulse, and
said it was beating hard.

We still believed.

Is Irrational Exuberance in Americans' DNA?

All of this raises for us an interesting question:
Was the recent economic crisis just one of those
cyclical events, perhaps set off by greedy financial
firms? Or did we cause it?

Consider at least two of the events that contributed to the near-Depression: Banks offered mortgages to people who could not repay them, and
people took mortgages they could not repay. But
did either party to those transactions truly think
the exchange was doomed from the beginning?

Why would they? We—whether we're the ones
working for a financial institution or the folks looking for a house—believe that tomorrow will be a

brand-new day. Sure, things look a bit grim, companies are laying people off, and our credit cards are maxed out. But that's today; tomorrow will be better. So optimists offer the mortgages, and optimists take them.

So if bad loans spelled our long period of doom, it's worth considering: Did they reflect a weakness in us or just remind us that too much of anything—including optimism—can be dangerous?

Economists also frequently lament a related issue: Americans spend too much and save too little. Benjamin Franklin and others, years ago, stressed frugality: Don't be penny wise and pound foolish; a bird in the hand is worth two in the bush; save for a rainy day.

But that was Benjamin Franklin, and he wasn't here to witness two world wars and see us become the greatest nation on earth, and then Ronald Reagan's Shining City on the Hill. He wasn't here to hear John Kennedy say we would have a man on the moon by the end of the decade and then witness one giant step on the moon just when he promised. He wasn't here to see us dominate the digitalization of the globe. And Franklin wasn't here to gather the confidence that comes from so many triumphs and so much growth.

So we believe, and then events confirm we should

have. And before long, there's a reason we don't save for rainy days: We don't believe in rainy days.

"Advertising sells one thing: happiness," reports Don Draper, the ad guru of AMC's hit TV show *Mad Men*. In announcing this, Draper echoes what a real-life marketer, Charles Revson, famously expressed. When someone suggested that his company, Revlon, made perfume, Revson corrected him. "In the factories, we make perfume," Revson said, "but in the stores, we sell hope."

Fortunately, both Draper and Revson find fertile ground in America. People who believe in major miracles, as we do, are even more apt to believe in lesser ones, like having thinner thighs in just seconds a day or becoming rich by working four hours a week. By our nature, we trust claims of "New and Improved!" because we believe in new and improved.

Skeptics—France has millions; the UK, too—are nearly immune to bold promises of a better life, and their advertising reflects it. Their ads are almost apologetic about asking for our patronage. But Americans listen to, and respond to, "New and Improved!" promises every day.

Americans believe, particularly in the greatness that surrounds them. It's what inclines Americans to another distinctive American trait: hyperbole, which infiltrates our advertising. We find few countries in which the language is so consistently inflated—the best, the best of all time.

The tall tale is a classic example, virtually an American invention. Our belief in ourselves and our greatness manifested itself once in a favorite tall tale of the Kentucky river men, including the famous Daniel Boone, who could "squat lower, jump up higher, dive in deeper, stay down longer, and come out drier than anyone."

Advertising hyperbole therefore hardly seems like hyperbole. The claims are grandiose and, judging by their repetition, effective.

So doesn't this seem the case? Being optimists, we believe grand claims and take our cues from the optimists who make them.

Three Masters at Tapping
Our Optimism

To see how our native optimism has been tapped in marketing, we will find no better examples than two men and one enterprise: a publisher, an author, and a retailer.

Before 1982, America's newspapers, in sober black and white, captured bad news: murders;

car, airplane, and stock market crashes; and the untimely deaths of the famous. After decades of leading cheers for their local teams, sports pages regularly castigated the stars and the teams' management and seemed to feature more crime reports involving players than scores of games.

Enough, Al Neuharth decided, and in August 1982, he gave us *USA Today.*

USA Today is Annie. It's a rosier view of "us," as the paper regularly refers to us. It talks directly to us and roots for us. To ensure we understand its cheery view, the paper abandons the traditional black and white. As we see with the iPod, the paper trades out the classic colors of serious adulthood—navy blue, charcoal gray, chocolate brown, and forest green—in favor of the bright Fisher-Price colors of our childhoods—red orange, goldenrod, light blue, bright green, and lavender blue. All of this deliberately suggests news as fun and play, typifying the paper that reasonably can be called "America's Cheerleader." *USA Today* knows: We believe.

To peek into one company that understands our optimism, click on Target.com—but click first on its competitor, Walmart.com.

Scan several pages of the Walmart site, and what do we see? Stuff: coats, swim suits, umbrellas, T-shirts. Where we don't see stuff, we see long lists of it: America's shopping list. What we don't see, however, are people; there are none. From, this, Wal-Mart makes it clear: It just sells stuff at good prices.

Now click over to Target.com. What do we see? Women, men, boys and girls, babies. Now notice something else. Yes, they are wearing stuff, but what we notice first is not their stuff but their faces: They are smiling. They radiate happiness and optimism.

In sharp contrast to models in fashion magazines, who strike the catatonic pose of the catwalk—"I'm too sexy for my skirt"—the models on Target's website strike the classic pose of the cheerleading squad for the high school yearbook photo. Each one appears to be posing for a tooth-whitener ad: She is beaming.

Target gets us; in marketing's top circles, the retailer is famous for getting us. Wal-Mart thinks we buy stuff, but Target gets it: Stuff sells well, but optimism sells even better.

Finally, there is a writer who gets us, and sells millions of books partly because of it. Malcolm Gladwell graduated from Harvard and writes for the *New Yorker*, which sends us two clues that he might be a liberal and intellectual, and therefore perhaps a pessimist. Is he?

Consider this startling, only-in-America section from Gladwell's introduction to *Outliers*:

What if we...began instead examining our own decision-making and behavior through the most powerful of microscopes. I think that would change the way wars are fought, the kind of products we see on the shelves, the kind of movies that get made, the way police officers are trained, the way couples are counseled, and on and on. And if we were to combine all of those little changes, we would end up with a different and better world.

Could Annie have said this better?

We love Gladwell because he tells interesting stories very well. But we also like how Gladwell makes us feel. He assures us that things will get better, that the sun will come out tomorrow.

He believes, and we love him because we do, too.

THE FORCES AND THEIR SOURCES

3. OUR EYES

In 2005, Coors launched a Belgian-style wheat beer called Blue Moon. It went nowhere—until Coors persuaded bartenders to change one thing: Serve Blue Moon in a glass with a slice of orange. Sales took off.

In 2008, Interstate Bakeries filed for bankruptcy protection. In 2009, it announced a revenue increase of 7 percent, which analysts attributed to just two changes: the introduction of whole-grain Wonder bread and, after twenty-five years without change, new packages for its iconic Twinkies, Ho Hos, and Ding Dongs.

In 2008, United States Beverage looked at the numbers for its Seagrams wine coolers and blanched. What was the problem? They sell their wine coolers in bars, but the coolers didn't look like they belonged there; they looked like wine coolers, a bit prissy. Seagrams repackaged them as Cooler Escapes in new beerlike bottles. That simple change boosted sales over 10 percent and helped Seagrams capture 36 percent of the wine cooler market.

In February 2009, Tropicana redesigned its orange juice cartons, eliminating its familiar symbol of a straw stuck into an orange. By April, sales had dropped 20 percent, forcing Tropicana to bring back the original packaging.

What happened in each of these cases?

Welcome to the Age of the Eye. In our new life of little time, hundreds of choices, and exceptional quality—this new life lived in a flash—there is one compelling force: the brightest flash.

What makes that flash? By definition, it's an image. It's design.

The indisputable importance of designers in this new century is the inevitable result of the last one. In those one hundred years, we learned to build things. Then we learned to build them faster, then smaller, then more efficiently. And then, with the influence of the quality movement and pressure from imports, we learned to build them at near–Six Sigma quality.

What was left for marketers to do? If they were computer manufacturers, they could try to dazzle us with lengthy descriptions of features we did not understand. As it became harder to create truly differentiated products, Apple and others realized a new possibility: the visually differentiated product.

We live in the age of the apparent. Design dominates this age because design works, and because our love of beauty is deep in our bones. It's deep inside us.

I. Our Need for Beauty

Lessons from Our Keyboard

Walk to your computer, open your word-processing program, and click on the bar marked "Fonts."

How many fonts do you find? The computer this book was first typed on contains eleven different fonts just under the letter A, from Academy Engraved to Arial Rounded MT Bold.

Of course, our escapades in fontography only start with those starting with A. You can have all those A through Z fonts in **bold**, *italic*, ***bold italic***, underline; you can outline it, shadow it, extend or condense it. You can display it in more than 164 possible sizes and an almost infinite range of colors.

This could go on, but you get the point. You no longer have something like a typewriter that prints one font, either Pica or Elite. You have a device for creating over a trillion different typefaces—just from the A typefaces alone.

If you still feel short on fonts, there's more. Buyfonts.com promises 1,600 fonts for Windows. If you still fear that some copycat may be using your typeface and you truly want to set yourself apart, there's an answer: Fonts.com, as of noon today, offers over 171,000 different fonts.

(If you've ever wondered about the force behind our world of a million fonts, it's Lloyd Reynolds, for years a professor of art history at Reed College in Portland, Oregon. In January 1973, a Reed freshman who had just dropped out after his first semester, inspired by the beautifully lettered posters on the walls throughout the southeast Portland campus, decided to audit a calligraphy course taught by Reynolds. Ten years later and inspired by Reynolds, that Reed dropout, Steve Jobs, helped design the first computer with multiple typefaces and proportionately spaced fonts: the Apple Macintosh.)

What is your computer telling you and telling all of us? We are visual animals.

We must be visual animals. The past decade's classic no-frills, cut-to-the chase CEO, Jack Welch, left GE identified with an extraordinary focus on quality, the company that made Six Sigma famous.

Yet lost in all his emphasis on the assembly line was Welch's emphasis on design.

But then, how could any perceptive CEO miss the rise of design? Teenage boys and our thirty-eight-year-old best friends were coloring their hair; men and women were making teeth whitening one of America's fastest-growing industries; fifty-five-year-old CFOs were adorning their bodies with tattoos; Sony's VAIO and Apple's candy-color iMacs, in Grape, Tangerine, Lime, and Orange, were demonstrating that a tool originally used to to crunch numbers had become a fashion accessory for millions of us.

Michael Graves had graduated from designing one of America's first icons of postmodern architecture, the Portland Building, to designing everyday products that appear in every Target store, everywhere—followed not much later by Philippe Starck, whose greatest fame had come from designing hotels far too expensive for the typical Target shopper.

Newspapers no longer were black and white and just offering the facts. Now images in primary colors had replaced a thousand words, in primary colors.

Starbucks, our newspapers, the jaw-droppingly massive screen that sprawls most of the length of the new Dallas Cowboys stadium—design and beauty are everywhere, and people stretch to afford it; design is the value-added feature. In Chile, as one emerging example, you can scan Santiago's crowded streets for hours before you spot a Chilean woman who does not appear to color her hair.

For men, this is relatively new. In the early 1960s, every man wore the same beige trench coat, dark gray suit, matching wool homburg hat, and patternless dark tie—think Don Draper on *Mad Men*. Men did not make fashion statements; they put on uniforms.

Then in rapid succession came the Kennedy assassination, the Vietnam war, drugs, dropping out, tie-dye, psychedelic color, and shoulder-length hair. In their wake, the uniform of The Establishment—the gray flannel suit, plain dark tie, and white shirt—was out, never to reappear. Today we are brands of one, making fashion statements that really are comments about ourselves.

Design is hard at work. And work it does, often in startling ways. If you approach someone today with a resume, for example, how will it be viewed? Can you afford to simply spew some well-thought-out words in minimally thought out Helvetica?

Let's see.

A young man named Andrew, an excellent high school football player with dreams of receiving a college football scholarship, presented his qualifications to evaluators. Suspecting that Andrew's style of presentation might affect the evaluator, a group of researchers presented his case in three different forms.

In the first, they typed out his statistics on a white sheet of paper.

For the second, they showed bar graphs.

For the third, they created a colorful Power-Point presentation that included the bar graphs, but which they animated to grow and shrink during the presentation.

How good a prospect for a football scholarship was Andrew? That depended.

The evaluators who viewed his sheet of paper rated him a 4.5 of a possible 7, or 64 percent.

The evaluators who saw his bar graph presentation rated him 12 percent better, at a 5, or 71 percent.

And the evaluators who saw Andrew's animated PowerPoint?

They gave him a 6: 86 percent. PowerPoint Andrew looked like a 33-percent better college football prospect than Plain White Paper Andrew.

Andrew's evaluators confirm for us again: We think with our eyes. Isn't that why Twinkies, Seagrams wine coolers, and Blue Moon beer seem to taste better today than they tasted two years ago, even though the formulas for those products haven't changed?

Staring at a Hand Ax: Our 400,000-Year-Old Urge

(For my understanding of the ancient examples of our love of art, I am particularly grateful to Harvard's Nancy Etcoff and her excellent book Survival of the Prettiest.*)*

When did we begin to love design? We started before our species started.

Even while they finished building their dwellings, fire pits, and other necessities, our ancient ancestors immediately started creating art. Some Paleolithic residents of what is now southern France painted hunting scenes in the Grotto Chauvet, the oldest cave paintings ever discovered—over 34,000 years old.

Now consider an even more remarkable discovery. In 1796 a farmer in Suffolk, England, named John Frere found several perfectly symmetrical and polished stone implements with sharp edges, which anthropologists immediately identified as hand axes. There is no practical explanation for their symmetry. If the axes' creators wanted just a tool, they would have kept one end of the rock blunt and the other sharp, and got on with their axing. But the creators went further; they made their axes pleasing to their eyes. They made tools for art's sake.

And they did this before our species evolved, before there was language, at a time when the tall males of their species—they were not even *Homo sapiens*—barely topped 4 feet tall. They did this over 400,000 years ago.

Almost as soon as we developed alphabets, we began to admire people who could draw those letters beautifully. We called this now-ancient art *calligraphy*, which literally means "beautiful writing." In Tibet, to be artistic was seen as holy, and great calligraphers were treated as nobility.

Then and now, beauty looks divine to us— literally.

Might our three basic needs be for food, shelter, and beauty? Archaeologists have found sticks of red ochre over 40,000 years old in South Africa; their only possible use was for makeup. In the Ancient Egypt section of London's British Museum, we come across a box. It's almost 3,500 years old. In it are an ivory comb and several items from the pages of *Glamour*: containers of makeup.

In January 2010, archaeologists from the

University of Bristol found an even older kit—an almost incomprehensibly older one. Digging in Spain, they found seashells containing lumps of a yellow foundation-type pigment and red powder mixed with a reflective black material. The powder turned out to be 50,000 years old. That meant this makeup had been used by people we long had regarded as only partly human: the Neanderthals.

Our love of beauty starts when life starts and springs up from below. Poor people first discovered and created paints, jewelry, and cosmetics. The Pueblo Indians were terribly poor and created gorgeous blankets. In impoverished rural India today you can find some of the earth's most spectacularly dressed people, in dresses of the richest reds and other vivid hues.

Any suggestion that design is window dressing or luxury finds no support in our history. If we do not crave beauty, why do archaeologists and historians keep finding it everywhere they look?

What *Sleeping Beauty* and *Beauty and the Beast* Taught Us

But what is good design? What do we love?

Again, let's go back to childhood. If someone

offered you several toys, which did you pick? If someone showed you photographs of several different people, which did you stare at the longest?

Show a baby a series of photographs, and he will focus far longer on several of them. Those photographs have this in common: They are the photographs of the people whom adults consider "most attractive."

But why do we love beauty? Is it partly because from these early years, we are told that we should?

We read *Sleeping Beauty*. She was the heroine of her story, a woman not merely beautiful but, by necessary implication, virtuous. Her archenemy—although Sleeping Beauty was too virtuous to hate anyone—was not merely evil but ugly. Evil and ugliness, we learned, arrive as twins.

Sleeping Beauty ultimately triumphs over ugliness and wins her reward for her happily ever after: the prince. But of course, she does not win just any prince. She wins the *handsome* prince.

Sleeping Beauty's ending is a classic one, almost identical to that of the *Beauty and the Beast*. Readers unfamiliar with *Beauty and the Beast* might assume that this tale marks the exception in which the beauty overlooks the beast's ugliness and lives happily ever after with it. In *Beauty and the Beast*, that is *almost* what happens.

In the climactic scene, Belle (the beauty) visits her family after promising the Beast she would return to him. The day of her promised return comes, but she does not, and with each minute that day, the Beast's heartache deepens. Fortunately for the Beast, Belle wears a magic ring that allows her to see the Beast's castle.

She looks in the ring, sees the Beast dying from his heartbreak, and races back to his castle. But she's too late. She shudders over the Beast's still body, then weeps. Like the ring, her tears prove magical; they revive the Beast. This being a favorite story in the Land of Optimists, America, the two live happily ever after, Belle and the Beast—don't they?

Not exactly. Belle's tears work such magical powers that they not only revive the Beast but transform him. He becomes what Belle deserves: a *handsome* prince.

Perhaps we love beauty, then, because adults for years have told us that we should.

II. What Is Beautiful to Us?

—

But what is attractive to us as children and later as adults?

First, repeated studies show that we love symmetry. As one example, we prefer faces whose left and right sides are closest to mirror images. The less the two sides of someone's face match, the less attractive we find it.

As babies, we stare longest at photographs of the people with the smoothest skin, just as we wisely prefer smooth surfaces for our toys. Smooth, seamless surfaces feel good, and rough ones hurt. Rough wood gives us splinters, and we learn.

Consider how we use the word "rough," and you see our bias: "They went through rough times." "Man, that's rough." "The edge looks a little rough; be sure you sand it." "Rough" estimates aren't accurate. In golf, you want to stay on the fairway and avoid the mess on either side of it: It's called the rough.

We love the smooth, and not just because it glows or sparkles. Perfectly smooth objects—the perfectly polished floors of our childhood, for example—appear spotless to us, and we hate spots. It's almost certain that we hate them because we link them to things that are unhealthy, even dangerous. We know to avoid people with measles or chicken pox, for example, and that even a small skin imperfection can be a warning sign of cancer or of something else that may need medical attention.

The spots we see often are specks of dirt, which breeds bacteria; spots make us sick. That realization is what drove Ray Kroc to not just create hamburgers and french fries that were identical in every McDonald's restaurant but to insist on spotless floors and antiseptic restrooms. McDonald's triumphed over a spotty institution that Americans everywhere called "the greasy spoon."

We see spotless and think healthy, and what appears healthy appears beautiful to us. We love rosy cheeks, red lips, full, shining hair: They look healthy.

In the mid-1990s, radio station producers had learned that for most American listeners, jazz was too random and unfamiliar, too spontaneous, not quite pretty enough. The producers knew that we would embrace something more melodic, something more flowing and seamless, too. They called it "smooth jazz."

The Circle and the Cube: The Shape of Beauty

In 1963, State Mutual Life Assurance of America—now Allmerica—needed help. The company had just acquired another insurance company and was concerned about the morale of the employees. So its marketing executives called Harvey Ball, the co-owner of its advertising and public relations firm in Worcester, Massachusetts, and asked if he could help.

It sounded like a mundane assignment, but Ball said he'd think on it. That afternoon, he returned to his drawing board and within minutes found himself drawing a perfect yellow circle with two circles and a semicircle inside: the now-famous smiley face. Thirty days later Ball received from his client a check for the entire amount he would make from his creation, $45.

Over the following years, his $45 creation would become a U.S. postage stamp, a symbol for Wal-

Mart, a button that in 1971 alone sold over 50 million copies, and an illustration of our love of simplicity and of the shape to which we are drawn from childhood: the circle.

The Lion King reminds us we are part of something special: the circle of life. We speak lovingly of our circle of friends. Our universe itself comprises circles within circles forming circles: the spherical planets, including ours, moving around the spherical sun in circular orbits.

Think of water, which we need to survive. How do we draw this very thing which gives us life? Asked to draw a picture of a source of water, we draw a circle.

We call a person we think is complete "well rounded." By telling contrast, someone behind the times was once called "square." Boxes are traps; when our thinking is stuck, we need to think "outside the box." If we break the law, we may be confined to a cell, another box. When we die, many of us are consigned to a box: "They put him in a box and buried him." The working space we most deplore is called a cube.

A woman with an appealing figure has curves. We do not use "curves" to describe a healthy-looking man, but the most appealing male shape has curves: the arced peaks of the biceps, the shoulder muscles and calves. What some call a nice butt and others a great booty isn't flat; it's rounded. The objects of special male fascination, the female breasts, are two circles: two orbs, each with a circle inside. The center of a male's fertility is rounded on the end, and the organs responsible for fertility are rounded, like balls.

The world's best designers realize this love of ours. Among the logos most often ranked as the world's twenty-five favorite, we find five circles (BMW, Mercedes, Firefox, Xbox 360, and Paramount Pictures), a stretched circle (Batman), a panda in an almost perfect circle shape (World Wildlife Federation), and three perfect circles (the symbol for Mickey Mouse). The five-circle symbol of the Olympic Games and the circular symbols of Starbucks and Target all rank with the most memorable and effective symbols of our time.

What about squares and rectangle? *None of the logos among the world's twenty-five favorite logos employs a rectangle, much less a box.* (Major League Baseball's comes closest, but its four edges are rounded.)

We love the curve and dislike the edge. Why might that be?

Again, look back to our childhoods and our ancestors. What are the first things that we see, the signals to us that we are safe and loved? The circle of a mother's eye, a circle within a circle—followed soon, as mentioned above, by the life-giving milk of a mother's breast, another circle within a circle.

Soon, what did we learn was safe and what was not? A rounded surface is smooth to the touch; an edge is not. The first great weapons and objects of our ancestors' fears were spears. When humans started making more lethal spears by shaping rocks into spear points, their deadly feature was a sharp edge: a point.

Points and sharp edges symbolize danger and evil. The devil in Christian tradition carries a trident: a spear with not just one point but three. The devil has pointed ears, not rounded ones. (By contrast once again, our symbol of belovedness, Mickey Mouse, has a perfectly round face and perfect circles for ears.) Verbal attacks are "pointed," and abrasive people "have an edge." The Lone Ranger's sidekick Tonto noticed the sharp edges of evil, too. "Kemosabe," he famously advised, "that man speak with forked tongue."

Contrast these sharp-edged symbols with those of Jesus and angels. What is an angel's signal characteristic? Wings, of course, with well-rounded ends—interesting, because not all birds have rounded wings. The other holy symbol is a circle: the halo. Jesus appears with one, but Christians are not alone in equating the circle with holiness. The ancient Egyptians depicted their gods Ra and Hathor with halos; so do the Chinese, Japanese, Tibetan Buddhists, and Hindus.

We love the circle and the curve and dislike the square and the edge.

The New Beautiful

In 2008, Philips Electronics conducted a study intended to measure the cost to American businesses of returned products. Their conclusion startled many people: The cost was $100 billion a year.

In years past, this news would have clearly signaled that America's quality movement had miles to go, that for all the talk about quality circles and Six Sigma, American business was still failing.

But in 2008, people reacted differently to the news, because it appeared the quality movement had shown some effect. Only half of the cost of the products we returned—$50 billion—could be attributed to defects in the products.

So what was wrong with the other $50 billion worth of products?

Nothing. We just couldn't figure out how to use them. *They were too complicated.*

Now, we might assume that our fellow consumers tried hard to learn about all those products before they returned them. We assume wrong again. These disgruntled buyers didn't spend days or even hours reading the manuals and tinkering with the product. They spent just minutes—*twenty minutes on average.* Then they surrendered.

Now, if a person disappeared into the rain forest in 1965 and only returned to America in time to read this Philips study, she wouldn't understand. She would remember the most complicated electronic product of the year, the 1965 RCA color television. It had an on-off switch, a color-control adjustment, a volume control, a channel changer, and the now-obsolete horizontal hold dial, to fix your picture when it started fluttering horizontally.

In 2008, our naive returnee from her forty years in tropical exile would discover a phenomenon of our time: feature creep. That's the clever expression for the tendency of manufacturers to add features to a product, in part so they can proclaim that it is new and improved. (Feature creep may have found its highlight in Microsoft's Word 2003 program; it featured 31 toolbars and more than 1,500 commands.)

Do we want better phones, or does that "better" just have thirty-five more functions we would never figure out, even if we could find a use for them?

We never figured out our VCRs before we had to replace them with DVD players, which we still haven't figured out. What chance do we have with a more fully functioned phone?

It seems obvious that the manufacturers believe they need to make complex phones to satisfy the tech heads. Are they just focusing on the Steve Wozniaks of this world, the tech wizard who created the first Apple computers and who probably owns a phone that can rotate his tires, feed his goldfish, and compose symphonies?

If they are, they're wrong. When asked about his relatively simple phone, the immortal Wozniak sounds like most of us: "I find my phone terrifying."

Even today's geeks feel overwhelmed by today's complexity.

As of this writing, these are the five best-selling books on Amazon:

Food Rules
The Help
Game Change
Dear John
The Kind Diet

These are the top five movies:

Avatar
Edge of Darkness
When in Rome
Tooth Fairy
The Book of Eli

These are the four most talked about products:

iPhone
BlackBerry
iPad
iPod

It's hard to look at those ten titles and four names and not be struck by their common trait: their brevity. The five top books average just 9 letters and just 2.2 syllables; the top movies average 10.4 letters and 3.4 syllables; the top products average 6 characters and 2.25 syllables.

Not one of these products has a name as long as Federal Express, which is "cognitively long" to our ears because it has five beats—five syllables—to pronounce. Only *Edge of Darkness* and *The Kind Diet* take as many as four beats, and half of those fourteen products have names with just two syllables. In 2000, Federal Express decided its name was too long and reduced it to the two-syllable FedEx, then took the added step of making it appear to be a single five-letter word. FedEx turned itself into an Apple.

Is something bigger going on here? Compare those five movies to the top-grossing movies of 1960, and you discover the 1960 titles used over 20 percent more letters and over 50 percent more syllables.

The move to brevity seems obvious. Is it deliberate, and is there a sound psychological reason for it? That is, are we more apt to buy a book or attend a movie with a short title or purchase a product with a short name? Is it that simple is beautiful to us?

The golf swing that today's golf fans find most beautiful is that of the South African player Ernie Els, whose nickname reflects the swing they love: They call him "The Big Easy." Fittingly, we use that adjective to describe an attractive woman's face; she is "easy on the eyes." Her face requires little effort to process, and that pleases and comforts us.

We love easy. In the early 1980s, popular music stations realized that aging Baby Boomers were tired of hard music; it sounded loud, strident. Fittingly, the radio producers called the offensive sound "hard" and labeled their more pleasing solution "easy listening." Easy is beautiful.

Our love of the simple is likely closely related to another of our traits: impatience. We are famous for being in a hurry. We might never think about this until we sit down to our first dinner in Italy, the country whose most famous classical writer, Baldassare Castiglione, insisted that one of the signs of personal greatness was *sprezzatura*—in our language, nonchalance. A nonchalant person does not rush or worry about time, and if the Olympics ever adds a nonchalance event, Italy's restaurant employees should be the early favorites.

In Italy, diners follow this routine: Arrive at 7:00; get a menu at 8; the waiter comes to take the order at 9 and delivers it at 10; he gets the dishes and dessert order at 11; brings the check at midnight; and returns the credit card receipt what seems like most of the night later.

We hurry; others don't. Procter & Gamble learned this when they introduced their popular time-saving Swiffer dusting products to Italy. Italian women wouldn't buy them. They think that a person should devote time to cleaning and dusting to get the best results; that cleaning means effort. Italians are hard to sell on dishwashers, too, for a similar reason— washing by hand is viewed as superior—and on washing machines, which they believe are hard on clothes. In the end, we see a cultural difference at work here. Americans trust machines and technology; Italians believe that humans are far superior. (Perhaps if our country had produced Leonardo da Vinci, Dante, and Michelangelo, we might view humans as superior to machines, too.)

Seeing this, P&G in 2009 repositioned Swiffer in Italy as products to use for the final touchups after cleaning and dusting. And as we probably guessed, Swiffer sales finally took off.

Time matters immensely to us. We invented the concept of own it now and pay later, thinner thighs in seconds a day, real-time Internet connections, the Indianapolis 500, land speed records and the Bonneville Salt Flats, the focus on new cars' 0 to 60 times rather than other traits, speed dialing, jaywalking and sane lanes, and microwaves. We don't even want to wait for brown skin; we flock to tanning booths and tanning sprays. And of course, we're the country that created fast food.

And simple means faster. Isn't our impatience, then, among the likely explanations for our love of simplicity?

Going with the Cognitive Flow

Look at the names of these four companies, and guess which two performed best—that is, which two experienced the greatest increase in the price of their stock over a one-year period.

Assume

Moughan

Cripta

Coumor

First, there's a very good chance that you got the right answers: Assume and Cripta. And the reason you got it right is that you looked at these companies the same way that prospective investors would. Subconsciously, at least, you decided that Assume and Cripta were better investments because the ease with which you could pronounce them made you more comfortable with them and confident in them.

Adam Alter and Daniel Oppenheimer in a June 2006 issue of the *Proceedings of the National Academy of Sciences* reported just that: Companies with easy-to-pronounce names outperformed those with harder-to-pronounce names. It actually went beyond that; Alter and Oppenheimer discovered that the companies with easier-to-pronounce ticker symbols also outperformed those with those with harder-to-pronounce symbols.

Once again, we are not always a thinking animal but an assuming one. We assume traits of a company from its name; we shortcut.

This Case of the Ticker Symbol isn't isolated. There's also the Case of the Exercise Programs.

Imagine that you decide to start a new exercise

program and are handed two program descriptions. The first is printed in the simple **Arial** typeface, the other in **BRUSH** font.

How long would you decide that each program would take? How easy and interesting would each program appear? Which one would you be most likely to start and continue?

Assuming you are like the people who were administered this test by Yale graduate student Hyunjin Song and Michigan professor Norbert Schwarz, your answer would be the Arial exercise program. It would seem shorter, easier, and more interesting even though—as you have guessed—it was identical to the Brush font program. The students estimated that the Brush font exercises would take almost twice as long to finish.

This once again shows that we often don't think; we assume. We somehow assume that an easy-to-read exercise program is easier to perform. We constantly take shortcuts, and the Looks or Sounds Easier is among our favorites. That is why the marketers of everything—and most obviously books, movies, and electronic products—are moving so clearly to shorter and simpler, and why *Lars and the Real Girl* sounds like a mouthful to us today, when less than fifty years ago we flocked to mouthfuls like *Butch Cassidy and the Sundance Kid, Close Encounters of the Third Kind,* and the high-grossing 1965 comedy *Those Magnificent Men in Their Flying Machines.*

Psychologists refer to these as examples of cognitive fluency, an odd expression because it lacks the precise quality it tries to describe: something that is easily understood. But despite that, their examples strongly suggest something deep within us: We take easiness as evidence of quality, simplicity as evidence of truth, and complexity as evidence that something is wrong.

The Masters of the New Beautiful

In contrast to feature-creep products, which literally cost tens of billions of dollars, consider the stunning success of their polar opposite.

The iPod Shuffle can claim the distinction of being simpler than a 1965 television—indeed, simpler than any electronic product ever made. This is what you can do with an iPod Shuffle:

You can turn it on and off.
You can turn the volume up or down.
You can skip to the next song or back to the previous one.

And you can set it to play songs in sequence
or choose them randomly.

That's it. That's all this thing does. And as one
mirthful observer noted, it sells like the wheel did
when it first came out, and for the same reason. All
the wheel did was roll, and all the Shuffle does is
play songs at different volumes.

What does this tell us about what Americans
want? Last year, we returned $50 billion worth of
products because, after just twenty minutes, we
decided they were too complex. And we spent
millions on iPod Shuffles, and more on the entire
line of Apple products that adhere to Apple's brand
platform: technology for people who don't like
technology and who don't want to spend more
than twenty minutes figuring theirs out.

Like the iPod, the FedEx name, and the simple
standard package offered on a Toyota Scion, Häagen-Dazs simplified. It reduced all its ingredients to
a simple five and introduced Häagen-Dazs Five.

Chipotle simplifies (and cleverly; by reducing its
burrito options, it moves the ordering lines faster,
thus turning over more customers). Its menu lists just
a few options, but the ingredients are so fresh that
customers are happy to have their choices reduced.

Costco simplifies; it's Costco's essence. Its competitor Wal-Mart carries sixty sizes and brands of

toothpastes; Costco carries four. Another rising star in retailing, ALDI, offers only 1,300 products total, a third of what Wal-Mart offers.

BoltBus simplifies. "A bus for a buck" could hardly be simpler, and that's the fare we can get if we're among the first reservers. Its loyalty program could not be simpler: Take eight trips, and the ninth is free.

Nintendo's Wii is so simple that analysts feared people wouldn't like it, with its simple motion-controlled wand and simple, childlike graphics. In an age when we love the simple, the Wii easily outsells the Xbox 360 and PS3. As happens at Chipotle, simplicity also adds profit. Wii games cost only $1.5 to $4 million to develop, compared to the $10 to $12 million cost of developing a game for the Xbox or PlayStation, and can go from concept to shipping at least twice as quickly.

But for sheer simplicity, does anything top Google? (And why don't more marketers learn from that and make their home pages simple and quick?) What do we see there? A logo, a box to type in, and two boxes, one of which reads "Google Search" and the other "I'm Feeling Lucky," giving us the chance to play.

If a company doesn't simplify, we do it for them. We learn there's "an app for that," and at this moment, there are 140,000 apps for smart phones.

With all that power at our disposal, how many does the average person use? According to the research firm Flurry, the answer is seven—the same number of digits we can remember in a phone number.

The wizards at Google, Nintendo, Apple, Costco, and Chipotle get it: We love the simple.

III. Our Eyes' Sheer Force: Five Studies

The Curious Case of Kensington High Street

Visitors went to Kensington High Street in London twenty years ago only if they could bear it. Once they arrived, they walked or drove at their own risk. Accidents and fatalities were constant, and the clutter was worse. Tom Vanderbilt, author of *Traffic,* called the area a forest—"a forest of signs." The look was a bad collage: streets and sidewalks suddenly would change from concrete to asphalt or brick for no apparent reason.

Kensington High Street was a mess.

The signs had become a forest because borough

officials reasonably believed that traffic warning signs accomplished their purpose: By warning people, they reduce accidents. To further ensure that safety, the borough had also erected guardrails on both sides of the streets and painted those familiar zebra-striped crosswalks to tell pedestrians where they could walk safely and where drivers absolutely had to yield.

The problem wasn't safety at that point. The problem for the Kensington merchants was that the area was so stuffed with signs, lights, guardrails, markings, and speed bumps ("Beware of Speed Bump" signs naturally followed) that it no longer looked like a community. That was a problem, because something dangerous was taking place nearby: a new shopping development that threatened to steal the Kensington merchants' business was being built.

Kensington's merchants adopted a reckless-sounding strategy. They decided to remove almost 95 percent of the signs. They eliminated the zebra-striped crosswalks and allowed pedestrians to cross anywhere. To expose walkers to even more risk but beautify the area, the borough even removed all the protective guardrails.

Everyone agreed: Kensington High Street now looked far more welcoming—but that could be a problem. The local shops might increase their store traffic, but the car and pedestrian traffic outside was certain to result in more accidents.

But it didn't. In fact, the opposite of what everyone predicted occurred. Pedestrian KSIs (Killed or Seriously Injured) dropped 60 percent.

This seems to suggest that the more civilized a place looks, the more civilized we behave in it. This rides on the hotly debated evidence of the success of Rudolph Guiliani's program of reducing graffiti on New York City's streets. When that campaign was followed by a reduction in crime, many argued the point: We behave more civilly in civilized-looking environments. And from the Kensington example, it appears that we also walk and drive more carefully in more civilized looking places. *Design changes how we act.*

Design changes not just our perceptions but our actions. Perhaps we should not repeat the old saw "Never judge a book by its cover," because covers matter; design alters how we see and feel. The cover *is* the book; *the package is the product.*

We probably find ourselves thinking that what is most remarkable about design is this: how superficial it *isn't.* Design, even the design of our neighborhoods, changes us—like the colors of our shirts, as we will see next.

Golfers in Red and Goalies in Black: How Color Changes the Game

Show a four-year-old the photo spread of Tiger Woods's winning celebrations of more than seventy professional tournaments, and she may ask you what Maggy Stemmer asked me when she saw that photo spread on my table at coffee one morning:

"Why does he have only one shirt?"

It's a reasonable question. In every photo, Tiger does appear to be wearing the same red shirt. It's a practice Tiger has followed since he began his professional career: He wears a red shirt on Sundays, the final day of every tournament.

One might assume Tiger is acting as a creature of habit, which he is. But there is more to Tiger's red-shirt fetish than mere habit; there is shrewd design.

To see why this might be true, let's leap to the 2004 summer Olympic Games. We likely are familiar with that favorite Olympics shot that NBC captures almost every night of the games. Our national anthem plays while the beautifully toned American athlete stands atop the victory stand—and then it comes: that little tear that trickles slowly down the athlete's cheek, right about when we hear "the bombs bursting in air."

As we watch, we imagine the athlete's feeling of triumph, the exquisite realization that his life's work has left him standing, literally, on top of the world. As it turns out, there was a lifetime of effort involved. But in many cases, there may have been something else: a red shirt.

After those 2004 Olympics, several anthropologists from Durham University in England studied the results of the games' four one-on-one combat sports: wrestling (Greco-Roman and freestyle), boxing, and tae kwon do. The researchers then isolated the contests in which, according to the sports' experts, the contestants were evenly matched. Blue, it turns out, was a good choice of uniform color. The blue-clad athletes fared well—unless they were pitted against athletes wearing red.

What happened then? In red versus blue matches, *the red-clad athlete won 60 percent of the time.*

The color of the uniforms cannot change the outcome of a contest, can it? And besides, wasn't that too small a sample? But color does seem to alter our behavior.

In 2009, Juliet Zhu, an assistant professor of marketing at the business school at the University of British Columbia, working with a doctoral student, ran a series of tests. They tested over six hundred participants on several problem-solving tasks, including solving anagrams and memorizing lists of words. Each task was performed against a red, blue, or white screen.

The color red, it turned out, worked like a green light.

Participants taking the test against a red background took off. They solved tasks that required attention to detail—remembering words or checking spelling—better and faster than when they were presented with the same task on a blue background. The phrase "red alert," then, may be remarkably apt; red does seems to make us more alert to details.

This also suggests that the ancient Egyptians and Chinese knew something. They practiced chromotherapy—cures using colors—and used red to stimulate people, physically and mentally. This stimulative effect that the Egyptians and Chinese found reveals itself in today's tests, which show that men are more attracted to women wearing red than any other color. This is why we often see red heels on a woman's CFM shoes—invitations to sex. This finding also makes the use of red for stop lights look like an insight, because a driver must be alert to any stop sign. The cost of missing one often is death. The likely danger in failing to respond to a green light, however, is the shock of hearing a sudden, loud bleat from the car behind us.

Does red clothing stimulate the person wearing it? Does it intimidate the opponent and explain why every golf commentator notices that Tiger's head-to-head opponents, every Sunday, always play horribly—"as if they are totally intimidated," the commentators usually add?

Do red uniforms worn in aggressive combat sports, like those four in the Olympics, prompt the judges to see the red combatant as more aggressive and therefore more deserving of the win?

If we still say that's very unlikely, let's consider hockey.

Hockey is a uniquely aggressive sport, a trait captured perfectly in a favorite joke: "I went to a boxing match and a hockey game broke out."

In hockey, fighting and other mayhem are tolerated but penalized: high-sticking, hooking, butt-ending, charging, elbowing, kneeing, kicking, slashing, spearing, and, of course, fighting. Reading hockey's list of penalties feels like reading a list of medieval battle techniques.

Now, penalties hurt a team. The penalized player must sit out at least two minutes of timed play and five minutes for "major penalties" and cannot be substituted. The penalized team must play a man short, sometimes even two short.

So here is an interesting thought. Might the color of their uniforms affect either the aggressiveness of teams, the number of penalties called against them, or both?

Well, we can start our research in Pittsburgh.

In 1979, the Pittsburgh Penguins were known

to be among the mildest-mannered teams of the National Hockey League. Only three NHL teams endured fewer minutes in penalties. After the season, the team management met, argued that the color black was getting big and that penguins are black, and decided to switch to black uniforms from their white and blue ones.

We can guess what happened. The fourth-least-penalized time in hockey became the *seventh-most-penalized team*—despite the fact that there were now four more teams in the NHL to slash, spear, and head-butt their way into those standings.

Was this just coincidence? If we think so, let's return to hockey one more time.

In 1978, the Vancouver Canucks had finished in the exact middle of the league for penalties; eight teams had more penalties, eight had fewer. At the conclusion of that season, the Canucks management decided to abandon their white uniforms for black ones.

We guessed it. The Canucks became thugs, apparently. Only two teams in the league were whistled for more penalties than the formerly peace-loving Canucks.

Even more than red, black signifies power. Judges wear black to signal their power over a courtroom and to deliver the implied command that no one in court can do anything that might be punished, literally, as contempt of court. Professors wear black robes to graduation, striped with black velvet sashes and black caps, to convey their authority. Executioners, the hooded men who worked the guillotines, and the Grim Reaper all wear black to signal their power over our final moments. And black, it turns out, figures in golf history, worn by a man who came before Tiger Woods.

Seen from behind, and if you ignore the gray in his full head of coal-black hair, Gary Player looks like an eighth-grader. He's 5 feet 8 inches and 165 pounds. Yet despite his small frame, Player won 164 tournaments worldwide, including all four of golf's major tournaments. It's an accomplishment that only Jack Nicklaus and Tiger Woods have equaled. Player also is known by his choice of attire: People call him The Black Knight.

Early in his career, Player began wearing only black clothes, offering an explanation we might expect from a small man: "Black makes me feel powerful." Perhaps it did. And perhaps it made his opponents, whom he vanquished a world-record 164 times, feel much less so.

Design changes minds, changes feelings, changes hockey players and referees, golfers and opponents. Its effect seems clear and almost certainly greater than we might ever have suspected.

The Mustang That Was Really a Bird

Within weeks of the car's introduction at the New York World's Fair on April 17, 1964, dealers were forced to auction their supply of Ford Mustangs because they had one car for every fifteen customers who requested one. On Memorial Day, it served as the pace car for the Indianapolis 500; that autumn it appeared in the classic James Bond film *Goldfinger*; by year's end, Ford had sold over three thousand cars a day and broken all American car-sales records. Four years later, the Mustang appeared in the Steve McQueen movie *Bullitt*—the promotional posters made it clear it was McQueen's costar—figuring prominently in what many regard as the greatest chase scene ever filmed.

Championed by Ford executive Lee Iacocca, the car created an entirely new class of American automobiles called the "pony class," sport coupes with long hoods and short rear decks, including the Chevy Camaro, AMC Javelin, and Plymouth Barracuda. But the Mustang's story goes back several years.

Five years before, Ford had introduced a car named for an animal that can travel at two-hundred miles per hour: the falcon. Partly the brainchild of Ford president and future U.S. secretary of defense Robert McNamara, the Ford Falcon initially sold in the millions, a huge volume for its day, but sales soon fell off. By the time Ford executives started considering the idea of a small sports car that would become the Mustang—the winning design was actually called the Cougar—Falcon sales had dropped so dramatically that Ford had surplus Falcon bodies in its plants.

Ten years later, the Falcon would disappear. Never iconic, low in price, and much slower than the predator for which it was named, the Falcon became a memory at best.

The different fates of these two cars seems destined to a reader familiar with automobiles. The Mustang seems an utterly different car than the Falcon, headed to a greatness that anyone could see would elude the Falcon. But it's hard to miss the irony: The Mustang was a Falcon.

The Mustang team took all those surplus Ford Falcon frames and suspensions and its tiny 170-cubic-inch engine and wrapped the Mustang's sheet metal around it. The Mustang changed the Falcon's skirt and hair style and offered add-ons like tachometers and special fuel gauges to enhance the impression of a high-performance car.

And that changed history.

Of course, not any change of skirt and hair style would have worked; Mustang's design was so inspired that it won the Tiffany Award for Excellence in American Design, a recognition no car had ever won.

Beyond its award-winning design, the Mustang's historic success also owes a great deal to several other influences stressed in this book. Management's faith in the car and its shape led them to make an unprecedented effort to plant the Mustang's name in Americans' minds. For the night of the car's unveiling at the World's Fair, they instructed their ad agency to buy every available time slot on all three of America's TV networks from 9:30 to 10 p.m., which in turn prompted *Time* and *Newsweek* to feature Iacocca and his car on its covers. So Mustang was the story that everyone heard, just like the Kobe Bryant story is the one every basketball player and fan hears today. Overnight, the Mustang was familiar.

The car also appealed to Americans because with just two doors and the Ferrari-like front end that project design chief Joe Oros requested, it was a sports car. It cried out, "Come in and play," and we love to play.

Finally, the name. The idea of a mustang speaks to one of our treasured American values, freedom: A mustang is an untamed horse running free. That name also evokes our western frontier, which is rich with meaning to us and the inspiration for what once seemed more than half of our television programs: *Gunsmoke, Have Gun—Will Travel, The Rifleman, Bonanza, Rawhide* (which launched Clint Eastwood), and *Wanted: Dead or Alive* (which launched McQueen).

The icon remains. For all the battles that Ford has endured and lost, its Mustang remains. Only one other Ford nameplate has been in production longer: Ford's F-Series pickup trucks. Ford's other sport car, the Thunderbird, came, went, and reappeared in a homage that failed to recapture that car's original aura.

Underneath, the Ford Mustang was a Ford Falcon. Yet the Falcon disappeared and the Mustang flourished, thanks to almost overnight familiarity, the promise of play, the implication of freedom, and a brilliant design that turned a mere bird into an icon that broke all the sales records of its day and that proves that even when they cost tens of thousands of dollars, we still buy books for their covers.

Vitaminwater's Sleight of Hand

One of several hundred bottled waters sold in America, Vitaminwater immediately throws us off

its marketing scent. Consider its name. If marketers wanted to create a breakout name for a bottled
water, they'd consider names like Aqua Energy,
Healthy H_2O, or Earth's Blessing. But if they wanted
to attract people who deplore the idea of marketing and to look like they weren't marketing to us
at all, they'd choose the most banal name possible.
They'd choose a name like Vitaminwater.

With that name chosen, where would marketers
distribute Vitaminwater? Not on the same shelves
with energy drinks like Gatorade, because Gatorade could drown it with advertising. Marketers
wouldn't want it to be with sweetened drinks,
either, because the Coca-Colas and Pepsis dominate those shelves.

But eliminating those two options leaves the
marketers with a dangerous one: battling with
several hundred waters on retailers' shelves. That
would pit them against the whizzes at Pepsi, who
sell Aquafina; the geniuses at Coca-Cola, who put
their mammoth resources behind their boutique
brand, Dasani; and the wizards behind that very
European-sounding water, Evian.

Even if the marketers could compete against
those giants, how would they battle the giant
and well-financed Nestlé, which markets six of
America's top-ten-selling waters, including Poland
Spring, Arrowhead, and Deer Park, which account

for almost one of every five bottled waters sold in America?

They could not wage their marketing war on television. Coca-Cola, Pepsi, and Nestlé would crush them with commercials if they showed their timid face on TV.

So where would they go to get traction? Straight to the grocery shelves. That space costs them nothing; it's an advertising medium they've already paid for.

How would they make the bottle their advertisement? If they slapped on a splashy, look-at-me label, they'd lose the magic and look like other waters. What do they do?

The marketers create an unpackage; they make a package that resembles a fact-packed nutrition label for a medically proven, vitamin-enhanced water. If they do that, many people strolling through the grocery aisles might sense that Vitaminwater is not a water but a medically endorsed daily antioxidant supplement.

They do that by printing the classic medical label, with a Helvetica-like typeface, in black and white.

Now as the brains behind Vitaminwater, marketers make one concession to packaging. They design two parallel rectangles that wrap around the bottle, the lower rectangle in white, the upper rectangle in a color—strawberry red, for example—to match the flavor of that particular water—strawberry, in that case.

Plain. Simple. But still a problem, perhaps. What makes this water different, other than vitamins, which no one will realize are in it if they don't notice the Vitaminwater bottle first? And they might not notice; dozens of different waters scream for attention from retail shelves.

What do the marketers do? They look at all those other bottles and ask what they share in common.

It's this: Waters are the color of water; they are colorless.

So what do the marketers do? They add color to Vitaminwater. By doing only that, they haven't tricked out the banal name or plain package, but the Vitaminwater bottle leaps off the shelf because in a clear sea, its waters leap out: They are red, orange, or blue. Browsers cannot miss Vitaminwater; it's red in a sea of clear.

By making these changes in creating Vitaminwater, the marketers haven't appeared to try too hard, so Americans cannot see the marketing cleverness behind the product. They notice this red water, the modest, marketing-free name, and their brains nudge them: "It's water, but with something more: vitamins! And it's medically proven."

It's brilliant: truly healthy water. It's brilliant

because it oozes simplicity. And it's brilliant because its brilliance, like David Copperfield's and Penn & Teller's and that of other magicians, is hidden from our view.

Part of Vitaminwater's brilliance, too, is that its executives know that we feel of two minds about brands. Brands attract us, but to some they can seem manipulative. Vitaminwater works because it stands out with no apparent effort and conveys its distinction from the other waters and drinks without saying more than two words: Vitaminwater—an unname with an unpackage.

Genius. Almost equal to that of the next man, who has changed this century.

The Man Who Crushed the Box

It came on midnight, August 1, 1998, but we need to go back further to tell the story.

From computing's early days—the first Altair, introduced to the world in *Popular Mechanics* in 1974—we often called a computer a "box." It seemed fitting. Everything was straight lines and sharp edges.

When Apple entered the computer market in July 1976, it created boxes, too. Even when it set out to revolutionize computing, with its heavily promoted

1984 introduction of the Macintosh, these innovators still chose a box, with an almost square screen and a rectangular mouse. Even the Mac icon that greeted us—literally in the first print ads, with the word "Hello"—resembled a square version of a smiley face, set inside a rectangular box.

The tyranny of the box became complete when Apple's future masters of design introduced their next breakthrough. The name they chose could not have been more fitting: They called it the Cube.

But thirteen years later, Steve Jobs and his Macintosh team were ready with something new: a computer so different that computing purists became even louder in dismissing Apples as computers "for the rest of them," by which these early adopter/whizzes meant "people without the bandwidth to operate a 'real' computer." Apple announced that it would reveal its masterstroke at exactly midnight, August 1, 1998. They called it the iMac.

The first iMac came in Bondi Blue, the color of California swimming pools. Seeing the success of this color, Apple then introduced Grape, Tangerine, Lime, Strawberry, and Blueberry iMacs, making it possible for customers to own a contradiction: a Blueberry Apple.

But while the color startled people, the shape surprised them more. The iMac was shaped more like a large half-egg, with the curved screen flowing to a rounded rear end. The ovoid was born; the sharp edge was gone. Every iMac team member knew what he had made, a near-clone of what many men consider the sexiest rear end on earth: that of the Porsche 911.

This curvy product changed the industry, as computer companies rushed to copy it. But they'd stuck with the box too long, oblivious to what Steve Jobs knew: We even make our hand axes beautiful, and we create art even when we are struggling to find food.

We crave aesthetics, particularly in an object as large as a computer. It takes up eye space in every room; if it's beautiful, it takes it up well, pleases us, and says something about us.

The iMac design beautifully incorporates almost everything we've talked about here: It is smooth, curved, symmetric, and famously easy to use, the product of the company that invented the phrase "user-friendly."

Not least of all, owning an Apple sent the Tiffany & Co. signal. Famously expensive, one's Apple signals to others, "I can afford it."

The Mac reflected Jobs's obsession with design. As a famous example of it, Jobs once insisted on changing all the hinges for the front doors of Apple's award-winning New York Apple stores. He said, "They don't look quite right."

Some will say, "Design is fine, but show us the money. What has Jobs's meticulous attention to design accomplished?" Being among the great percentage of Americans who don't own a Mac, these doubters probably assume Macs make up not more than 15 percent of the market. Actually, their market share is lower: around 10 percent. But this misses the point. Macs dominate the high-margin end of the computer market; 74 percent of the money spent on computers costing over $1,000 is spent on Macs.

Plus, the Mac merely acted as Apple's Trojan Horse. It stalked in and brought Apple's "digital lifestyle products" along behind it: the iPod, iTunes, and the iPhone, each obsessively designed and each integrated with the Mac, which makes the Mac even more attractive.

What has Jobs's meticulous attention to design accomplished? A year after introducing the Bondi Blue iMac, Apple was worth around $5 billion. Today it is worth $171 billion—more than Google, Cisco, Sun, and every other company in Silicon Valley and all but two other companies in all of America. And today, Steve Jobs himself is worth what all of Apple was just months after introducing Bondi Blue: $5 billion.

On November 23, 2009, *Fortune* magazine named its CEO of the decade; it was Jobs. Later, it would name his company the company of the year for the third consecutive year. In the November-issue articles saluting him, the word "design" and words related to it, like "aesthetics," appeared fifteen times. His company has suggested to the rest of the world—one should say shouted to us—the direction of this new century: It is in the direction of our eyes. We think with them.

Steve Jobs is the CEO of the decade, and it is accurate to say this: He got there by design.

He appeared to be a gruff British prime minister with no use for mere design, but Winston Churchill once made a perceptive observation about the unusual influence that design has on us: "People shape buildings, and then the buildings shape people."

Our creations change us. McDonald's creates fast food, and just seeing its logo causes us to be less impatient and to read faster, if we are to believe the credible-sounding research of Sanford DeVoe and Chen-Bo Zhong. Our designs and images change us in ways we'd never guess.

In this section, haven't we seen just how true that is, of streets, computers, hockey jerseys, wrestling uniforms, wine-cooler bottles, Twinkies packages, and ordinary Falcons transformed into iconic Mustangs? We respond to design, particularly when

it understands our love of beauty that we demonstrated 400,000 years ago. If something is smooth,
spotless, symmetrical, simple, easy, and familiar,
it works even more. It makes bar patrons drink
wine colors, people buy more Twinkies but fewer
cartons of Tropicana orange juice, and makes water
drinkers choose Vitaminwater over more heavily
advertised competitors. It helps make Steve Jobs
worth $5 billion.

And it certainly seems to prove that this is the
Age of the Eye.

UNTHINKING: THE ROAD AHEAD

━━━━━━━━━━━━

I. Looking Back to Our Future

———

We're in a breezy Boston café, but it could be Every Coffee Shop, 2010, glancing around at the college juniors, recent retirees, and twenty of America's 22 million cubeless workers.

Judging by the many rumpled *Wall Street Journals* and *Boston Globes,* they look well informed. We notice at least one laptop per table, beaming into the transfixed eyes of its owner. They reflect two habits of Us, 2010: We sip coffee and guzzle information.

These coffee klatchers are in the know, another passion of our time. We have to know—first, if possible. In the age of information, not knowing is a form of not belonging.

These Bostonians are the products of decades of trends in the United States. We have tracked these trends, wondering where they will take us. But looking around this coffee shop, what do we see?

We see men in polo shirts, button-down long-sleeved shirts, khakis and jeans. We see Adidas and Puma running shoes, leather loafers, and crew neck sweaters.

In 1964, what would we have seen? Polo shirts, button-down long-sleeved shirts, khakis and jeans, Adidas and Puma running shoes, leather loafers, and crew neck sweaters.

A teenaged boy pulls up in a Mustang wearing Fred Perry tennis shorts; the fellows heading to work sport two- and three-button suits and black and brown lace-up shoes; to ward off the sun, four people are wearing Ray-Bans. It is déjà vu 1964 but with fewer silk ties.

This is where our trends have taken us: forward to our past.

In the 1970s and 1980s, we stood in line for *American Graffiti* and made *Happy Days* and *Laverne & Shirley,* set in the 1950s and 1960s, our hit television shows. Thirty years later, we return to a time most of us regret: the 1970s.

Austin Powers reprises and spoofs the Bond and spy films.

VW introduces the Beetle, this time with a flower vase on the dashboard.

Chrysler introduces a car that looks like the cruisers that protected Al Capone's gang as they pillaged Chicago in the 1930s.

Bell-bottoms come, go, and return, with hip-huggers close behind.

The *Globe* entertainment section notes that 2009's number-one-grossing concert of 2009 was Britney Spears'. It doesn't mention that 1999's was Britney Spears', too. AC/DC and Metallica are in town, Korn seems perennial, and the Rolling Stones, gathering moss as they near seventy, are this decade's top-grossing band. *The Rolling Stones?* At seventy-three, Tina Turner announces her final final last final tour.

Once there was hip-hop. Most of us think it's new. But hip-hop came, declined, then returned: instant retro hip-hop.

In the 1950s, futurists made us confident that by 2000, we would be wearing jumpsuits and jet-packing through the skies to work. Downtowns would be car-, slum-, and beggar-free. *The Jetsons* showed that our rooms would be stripped of everything but the essentials, that robots would vacuum our floors, and that we often would wear space helmets. Our clothing would be free of buttons, perfectly fitted, and ready to fly. In 1968, the movie *2001: A Space Odyssey* envisioned regularly scheduled passenger space travel; it's still not here.

In Epcot-like fantasies, we were shown the car of 2000. It still has not arrived. Car sound systems, however, work much better, featuring more speakers than anyone used to own in an entire house.

How much have we changed? Our electric power, ships, and planes are driven by technologies that are 130, 110, and 80 years old, respectively. Television is nearing hundred years old, and the truly transformative technologies of refrigeration, air conditioning, and indoor plumbing are almost as old or older.

These innovations come, and we overestimate their disruptiveness. We were told television would kill radio and movies and that TiVo would kill television. They all flourish. We were told that the Internet would kill print. In 1970, 174.5 million people subscribed to magazines; in 2008, the number reached 324.8 million. In this Boston coffee shop at 2:50 p.m., we can scan the room and count: Seven people are working on computers, four of them are on the Internet, and five people are reading today's *Boston Globe*.

Some trend spotters assure us that social networking sites like Twitter will transform our lives and the marketing of products. Coors, Panera, Ray-Ban, Pampers, Domino's, and BMW all set up Twitter sites, and as of this writing, their total number of followers exactly equals the population of Bisbee, Arizona.

If there are so many trends, why are we still the way we were? If we are changing so much, why is it so hard to tell?

On June 10, 2007, the *New York Times* reported another new trend: the *decline* in the online sales of products. Here was its evidence for the decline:

> Forrester Research, a market research company, projects that online book sales will rise 11 percent this year, compared with nearly 40 percent last year. Apparel sales, which increased 61 percent last year, are expected to slow to 21 percent. And sales of pet supplies are on pace to rise 30 percent this year after climbing 81 percent last year.

This story is a trick. Let's start over and put on our own reporter's glasses and decide the actual trend was the continued *growth* of online sales. We could take the exact same data and write:

> Sales in all online categories are up, well ahead of sales trends in the general retail market. Online book sales are expected to rise 11 percent this year, after rising 40 percent last

year. Apparel sales in stores are up 3 percent but have soared 21 percent online. And pet supplies are the big winner: They're up 30 percent this year—*six* times the increase in sales in retail outlets.

Why didn't the *Times* report *that* story? Money and fame. The three biggest stories in journalism of the past thirty years hint at that: Janet Cooke of the *Washington Post* winning a 1981 Pulitzer Prize for the riveting story of an eight-year-old heroin addict; Stephen Glass winning fans and the adoration of his fellow *New Republic* editors and writers with his captivating stories between 1995 and 1998, a story itself so compelling that it was made into the movie *Shattered Glass*; Patricia Smith of the *Boston Globe* being named a 1998 Pulitzer Prize finalist for column writing.

A thread runs through those three writers' stories: They were fabricated. The writers' ambitions to write award-winning and career-making stories overcame their appreciation for the truth. But that temptation surrounds every media outlet today, posing the question of this decade: How do we get eyeballs?

We see the temptation in this *New York Times* story, too. The writer didn't write "Online Sales Continue to Grow" because that wouldn't be big

news; it would merely continue an old trend. Newspapers must write news; no news, no eyeballs. So
as Cooke, Glass, and Smith did, the headline writers and reporters succumb to temptation.

Even august-sounding publications like the *Harvard Business Review* feel this urge. We see this
vividly in its feature "The 20 Breakthrough Ideas
of 2005."

The first surprise: There were twenty huge ideas
that year. Have we had twenty in this decade?

Our suspicions deepen when we scan the too-
clever headlines for the ideas: "The Velcro Organization," "Everyone into the Gene Pool," and
"Blog-Trolling in the Bitstream." But it is the *Harvard Business Review,* so we assume it's credible,
maybe even definitive. So we start with "The Velcro Organization." Here's its big idea as summa-
rized by *HBR*'s editors:

> When your customers are located around the
> world, it's not enough to have effective, effi-
> cient functions. You also need to know the
> people and relationships that work in particu-
> lar locales.

Okay, we say: only nineteen Big Ideas.

Big Idea #17 advocates midcareer sabbaticals for
workers, to reenergize them and their companies.

Many readers in large companies have heard this idea for years, often from their own lips.

The editors save their remarkable best for last: It's Big Idea #20, and it must rank among the truly ironic ideas of 2005 and beyond, given its context in this article on the 20 Big New Ideas:

"Be skeptical of anything touted as 'new.'"

Everyone reports trends because we love to read about them. Why? We are optimists, and optimists believe in change. We believe that in every day and in every way, we are getting better. That belief has created entire industries to satisfy our appetite.

But the media's reporting of nontrends finally irritated one writer so much that he decided to expose it. In August 2003, *Slate* magazine and Jack Shafer began a regular feature with the perfect title: "Bogus Trend of the Week Award."

Bogus Trend began with a report on the "decline" in online sales, followed by reports on nontrends including eating locally grown food (supported entirely by anecdotes from people found buying locally grown items in stores); men who own cats; booming evangelical attendance (it wasn't happening); a purported trend among people leaving areas threatened by global warming; and increases in shoplifting, a "trend" apparently planted by retailers to make shoplifters more afraid of the legal consequences, among many others.

Are there real trends afoot? If there are, the false ones outnumber them, as this Boston coffee shop reveals. The old saw remains true: The more things change, the more they stay the same.

And the more we want to see trends, the more we will hear about them—whether they exist or not.

Today's smart marketers realize that most trends are small: blue being the new black, for example. They also know something else; once we spot even a small trend, we're too late. These marketers have a term for it: That tiny trend already is "post peak."

These marketers also know that these tiny trends come and go, but humans barely change over centuries. Like the Neanderthals, we still wear makeup and prefer tools that look good; yesterday's lovely hand ax is today's OXO can opener. Our loves don't change, and the best marketers know that. So they don't follow trends; like us, they follow our hearts.

II. THE EULOGY AND THE SIX-INCH NAIL: THE STARTLING POWER OF EXPECTATIONS

In the fall of 1953, Californian Denny Hansen arrived on the campus of Yale University in New Haven, Connecticut. His blond buzz cut, broad shoulders, and bright white smile made him the Sun God of gray New Haven.

By Denny's junior year, almost everyone who knew Denny assumed he would one day be president. His classmates often played a favorite game: Which man would serve which cabinet post in the Hansen administration? They agreed that Denny's worst career case would be as secretary of state, a step down but an accomplishment.

That was the least Denny could expect, particularly

after he was chosen for the prestigious Rhodes Scholarship. Yet that Rhodes announcement wasn't even the highlight of Denny's senior year. That came weeks later, when Denny Hansen's name and face became known to over ten million Americans.

In the spring, two editors at *Life* magazine, one of America's most popular publications, decided to cover Yale's graduation. Hearing about Denny's "golden boy" angle, they decided to focus on him.

Reading the article that sprawled over several pages, with stunning Albert Eisenstadt photos, *Life*'s readers soon learned that Denny was a young man of "astonishing completeness." They were reminded of that just five months later when, seeing a "Where Are They Now?" angle, the magazine dispatched a team to Oxford to see how Denny was doing.

He was doing great. Ever the all-American boy, he asked the dons not to assign him texts written in German and Latin. At night, his fellow Oxonians' favorite outing was to Oxford's seven-hundred-year-old tavern, The Bear Inn, where they downed ale and bitter. Denny ordered Ovaltine and orangeade. His new classmates found him as radiant, too; they called him "ebullient."

And then…Like many great stories, Denny's takes a twist. Thirty-four years later, in the coastal town of Rehoboth Beach, Delaware, neighbors of a home owned by Scott Thompson called the police.

"Something strange next door," they said. Two officers immediately drove to Thompson's house and noticed smoke coming from the garage. They broke in.

They found a Honda with its engine running. One officer rushed to open the driver-side door and immediately noticed a body lying on the passenger-side floor, then spotted a frying pan and hardback book propped on the accelerator.

The Golden Boy's body was blue.

This was a tragedy that only Denny's friends ever would have heard were it not for another former Yale student and estranged friend of Denny's: the author Calvin Trillin.

Almost everything about Calvin Trillin looks rumpled. His shoulders are rumpled, his walk is rumpled, his brow and chin are rumpled. Even his rare Mona Lisa smile looks rumpled. It is as rumpled as his frown, which, judging from Google images of Trillin, represents his favorite pose. There is no photographic evidence that Calvin Trillin has teeth.

What Trillin does have, despite his rumpled-ness and perhaps augmented by it, is wit. Trillin makes people laugh for the same reasons that Jackie Mason once did and Steven Wright still does. These men look dour. Their moods are so gloomy and rumpled—Wright's hair looks to have been groomed by electricity—that their wit works on one of our great pleasures: the power of surprise. As when we see a sad clown face, we are surprised when sad-looking men do or say funny things, and Trillin says funny things often.

Hansen's death startled Trillin. He had not heard from or about Denny for years but often noted his surprise after another year passed without hearing something of Denny's fame, somewhere. So after the small memorial ceremony for Hansen, Trillin began writing Denny's poignant story.

On April 1, 1993, the result, *Remembering Denny,* appeared. This turns out to be yet another story, not of dashed expectations but of expectations generally, and how they distort the lenses through which we see. It begins in the American Midwest, days after Trillin's book was released.

Trillin's publishers had arranged for a book tour, with one of his first stops in Minneapolis. On a Tuesday afternoon just days after April Fool's Day, a large crowd—at least seventy—squeezed into a musty-smelling room on the University of Minnesota campus. Minnesotans love to read, partly because their long, cold winters coop them up indoors, so most of those seventy eager people knew Trillin from his witty contributions to the *New Yorker* and thirty years of articles in the *Nation*.

Trillin entered the door and walked to the oak podium. The Minnesotans clapped enthusiastically while they noted that, as usual, he looked rumpled. He began to tell Denny's story. Like that story, the story of Trillin's presentation has a surprise ending.

Trillin read a brief passage. There were giggles. He read another poignant passage. More giggles, again and again for twenty minutes. The Minnesotans loved the gifted humorist, his dry wit brilliantly on display. But there was a problem.

Trillin was not trying to be funny. He was not even being funny by accident; he was saddened and mystified by the death of his friend. But the audience clearly found Trillin very amusing. Why?

Remembering Denny was so new that few audience members had seen it, much less read their copy. So when they heard Trillin read from his new book, they laughed for one reason. *They laughed because they expected they would.*

The man speaking was Calvin Trillin, after all, and Trillin is funny, and so he was funny—even though he wasn't. As we've heard all our lives, "His reputation preceded him."

Everything has a reputation that precedes it. But Trillin's experience suggests that reputations do more than set our expectations. *Reputations change the entire experience.* They perform like the reputation of Apple CEO Steve Jobs. As people around Jobs often say, his aura sets off a "massive reality-distortion field."

We experience what we expect. If we see a van Gogh for the first time, we are stunned by the force of *Starry Night*—unless we are from a circle that regards van Gogh as a kook who chopped off his ear and painted works with a perspective that was warped, literally and figuratively.

We think heavily footnoted books by professors sound thoughtful, well-reasoned, and correct. We expect a movie with Will Ferrell or Matthew McConaughey to include a scene where the actor appears without a shirt. Years later, we recall that he appeared shirtless in that movie, even though he didn't. We remember what we expected to happen, even if it didn't.

Psychologists refer to this under the heading expectancy theory, which in turn relates to the better-known idea of placebo effects. Repeatedly, we taste what we expect, see what we expect, experience what we expect to experience.

But it gets even stranger than this. If we think something will do something, it often does. If we think it makes our hair grow or our teeth white, our hair sprouts and our teeth whiten. Many products and services have the effects they promise— *perhaps even before we actually use them.*

*   *   *

Dr. Ellen Langer has broken ground in the world of psychology, the first female tenured professor of psychology at Harvard. Her work has deeply influenced our understanding of how we make decisions, and among her many interesting discoveries was one she made in 2006.

Langer wanted to discover how much of the benefits of exercise might simply be in our heads. To accomplish that, she solicited the help of eighty-four Boston women between eighteen and fifty-five who worked as housekeepers in seven Boston hotels.

Langer told the workers at four of the hotels that their housekeeping work was good exercise and "met the guidelines for a healthy, active lifestyle." She told the other housekeepers nothing.

Then she asked all eighty-four workers to record their daily activities, which later allowed Langer to see that the housekeepers' work activities didn't change during the four weeks she observed them. They cleaned fifteen rooms a day, up to thirty minutes for a single room.

So we had two identical groups but for one difference: One group was told that its work was good exercise and the other group wasn't.

What happened? The housekeepers in the informed group reported their lives were healthier than those in the uninformed group. But it wasn't just what they said; they *were* healthier.

The members of the informed group lost an average of two pounds and 0.5 percent of their body fat and saw their systolic blood pressure drop 10 percent. The other women showed no such changes.

Doesn't this strongly suggest that if we think it is, it becomes? That if our minds decide our work will make us healthier, that thought alone makes us healthier?

Our expectations change us, inside out.

Late in the fall of 2008, some lovers of Italian food arrived at the Provence Restaurant on Bleecker Street in the West Village section of New York City. Surrounded by symbols of Tuscany (curious, considering that Provence is in France, almost 1,000 miles from Tuscany), the diners were treated to the chef's latest creation, a pasta called Tuscani.

As foodies like Calvin Trillin know, better restaurants make their pastas from scratch, use only breast meat, and grate the Parmesan cheese at the diner's table to ensure the freshest taste. Knowing this instinctively at least, the diners at Provence braced for a delicious dinner.

The Tuscani came and dazzled the diners. "Marvelous!" one proclaimed, and others joined in. They found that the ingredients and presentation were worthy of this fine Italian restaurant.

There was a problem, as some of you know. The Culinary Institute of America–trained chef at Provence had not prepared the pasta; the minimum-wage cooks at Pizza Hut had.

Pizza Hut's chef popped out a Tuscani Pasta with Meaty Marinara Sauce (another mistake; by definition, marinara sauce has no meat). Its key ingredients were egg yolk powder, "cheese flavor," xanthan gum, meat from chicken ribs, and preservatives. The reality—these ingredients—should have disturbed the diners, but we often cannot see, taste, feel, or hear reality.

The diners' experience, captured on thirty hidden cameras and edited into a Pizza Hut commercial that began airing in March 2008, was—well, they tasted exactly what they expected to taste in this chic New York eatery.

Pizza Hut was recycling an old idea. Decades earlier, Folgers had tried to coax Americans into drinking its freeze-dried instant coffee with a similar ad, filmed in famous American restaurants, including the Blue Fox in San Francisco and New York's Tavern on the Green. Just as the Tuscani Pasta samplers would decades later, the diners at these famous restaurants pronounced their test-tube coffee "marvelous." It tasted as if the beans had just arrived from Colombia.

The two ads worked in one sense: They demonstrated that over the course of forty years, we have not changed. We experience what we expect to experience. We expect Calvin Trillin to sound witty and the Blue Fox's coffee and Provence's pasta to taste delicious. And they do—*even when they don't.*

Our expectation, shaped by our entire view of a brand, doesn't merely influence our experience. It *is* the experience.

Our expectations, many of them arising from the "brand" we have in our mind, alter our experiences. But just how much?

Incredibly. We can reach this conclusion by starting with another famous ad campaign: The Pepsi Challenge. These commercials were based on a sensible proposition. Whenever researchers at Pepsi conducted blind taste tests with unmarked cups of soda, almost two-thirds of the tasters preferred their cola to Coca-Cola's. Voilà! A great idea for an advertising campaign!

Why not just film these taste tests so that people everywhere will see that Pepsi tastes better?

So they did. Millions saw the ads. And afterwards, those same millions kept right on drinking their beloved Coca-Cola.

Somewhat curiously, the Coca-Cola people in Atlanta knew that the Pepsi people in upstate New

York were right. In Coke's blind tests, people preferred Pepsi's taste, too, but still chose Coke.

Voilà! Another great marketing idea!

What would happen, the Coke folks reasonably
wondered, if we made Coca-Cola taste even better?
What if we made it so that people in blind taste
tests would like us even more than Pepsi? We will
flatten Pepsi!

Thus was born the Seward's Folly of modern
marketing, the new Edsel: New Coke. Reconsti-
tuted, more delicious than old Coke, more delicious
than old and new Pepsi, New Coke won blind taste
test after blind taste test.

The people at Coca-Cola were merely repeating the mistake of the Pepsi folks, a mistake that
rested on what now looks like a comically glaring
error: In real life, there are no blind taste tests. We
do not drink just any cola; we know what we are
drinking.

There is even more to it than that, as a fellow
from Dr Pepper country would soon demonstrate.

In Waco, Texas, Dr Pepper's home, we find the
Baylor College of Medicine and its Human Neu-
roimaging Lab. The lab's director, Read Montague,
had become intrigued with the phenomenon of
the mind's influence on the body. He started to
ponder the Pepsi paradox: Why do people say they
prefer Pepsi's taste when they don't know what

they are drinking, yet still prefer Coca-Cola's taste when they do? Does the mere knowledge in our brain—"This is Coca-Cola"—actually change how we experience it? Does the very *idea* of Coca-Cola affect our sense of taste?

Montague decided to find out. He performed a new Pepsi Challenge while he scanned the brain activity of the tasters. Once again, more tasters preferred the unmarked cup that held the Pepsi. One part of the tasters' brains especially loved Pepsi: their ventral putamens, one of the brain's reward centers. This part of the tasters' brains fired five times stronger when they tasted the Pepsi but didn't know it was Pepsi.

So The Pepsi Challenge was right. Our brains really *do* like Pepsi's taste more—when it doesn't know what we are drinking.

So Montague added another twist. Before each taster took a sip, Montague told him which brand he was tasting. Guess what happened? Now the tasters overwhelmingly preferred Coke.

We say, that's no surprise; we love what we love. Tell us that something is our beloved Coke, and we will tell you we love Coke.

But there was more to it than that. It wasn't just that the taste testers preferred their old favorite, Coke. *Their brains acted differently, too.* Their medial prefrontal cortices, the portion of the brain

strongly involved with our sense of self, fired cra-
zily. The word and idea of Coke apparently strongly
links to our sense of ourselves. It appears that we
like Coke because it makes us feel better about
ourselves. It's not just our taste buds that like Coke.
Our brains like it, and our brains change what we
taste, see, feel, and hear.

Montague's discovery did not surprise people who
had been involved in the testing of hair-restoration
products. In controlled tests, 40 percent of Group A
reported that Extra Strength Rogaine had produced
for them "significant hair gain." Group B had even
better luck, with 60 percent reporting hair gain.
There was a small problem, however.

Group A had not been given a hair-restoration
product. They were a control group! They'd been
handed a vial of oil and water. Yet they saw hair!
The Rogaine brand name attached to their vial convinced them that it would grow hair, and so that
"Rogaine" grew hair. The *idea* of Rogaine made
them see hair.

And then there's the oddest case of all: the case
of the six-inch nail.

Just after New Year's Day 2010, a twenty-nine-
year-old British builder working at a building site
west of London jumped from a landing and landed
on a six-inch nail with such force that the nail

penetrated his boot and nearly came out the top. Seeing his extreme pain, his coworkers called emergency services, and a car soon rushed the young man to an emergency room.

Because moving the nail even slightly caused the man enormous pain, the ER doctors quickly sedated him with midazolam, which is used before surgery to induce drowsiness or unconsciousness. It illustrates the severity of the young man's pain that the doctors also administered fentanyl, a painkiller often prescribed for terminal cancer patients that is one hundred times more powerful than morphine. (Fentanyl had earned some notoriety just months earlier when investigators found bottles of it in Michael Jackson's home after the singer's death.)

With the patient sedated and his pain controlled, the doctors then proceeded to carefully remove his work boot. When they finally were able to remove it, they discovered something startling: The nail had passed cleanly between the builder's toes. There was no injury at all.

What happened there? An example of the nocebo effect, one of the more bizarre examples of how our expectations change our perceptions and feelings. If we think we have a nail in our foot, it can hurt so much we need a near-lethal drug to reduce our agony.

Repeatedly we see it: What we expect changes

what we feel. We taste a Provence pasta or a Coca-Cola, or sense a nail in our work boot, and we experience what we expect to. We experience not things but our ideas of those things. Our brains fool our bodies, just as our bodies often trick our brains.

So better or worst aren't qualities that exist in the world; they are in our brains—our bewildering, erratic, more-complex-than-the-entire-universe brains.

This in turn dictates the first principle of marketing in the twenty-first century. Marketers cannot merely develop great products and services; they must develop, nurture, and manage great expectations.

There is mounting evidence that for all the expectations that they create, superior brands, far from delivering superior results, deliver only average results. The latest evidence comes from financial services, the beleaguered whipping boys and girls of the recession.

Assigned the task of taking public her new software company, Blue Mongoose, Emily Peters immediately makes a short list of three banks to help manage the IPO: JP Morgan, Citigroup, Wells Fargo. She lists these three banks because they are banks almost every CFO lists: They dominate American finance. If she chooses a less-reputed investment bank and her IPO fails to achieve its target price, Emily's next act as Blue Mongoose's CFO may be the swift updating of her résumé. Just as for years executives have learned the old business saw "No one ever gets fired for choosing IBM," no one second-guesses a CFO who chooses one of these firms.

Emily assumes, as most readers do, that these companies represent the best and the brightest in banking. She assumes that each of these banks is most likely to get Blue Mongoose the best target price for the IPO, the ultimate measure of going-public success.

Does she assume right? The data suggests she doesn't. As James Surowiecki pointed out in a recent *Wall Street Journal* article, the big banks have proven no more successful at managing IPOs than the comparatively tiny banks whom the Emilys of America overlook—indeed, whom the Emilys never call on. These big banks are the great brands of their industry, but in managing IPOs, their performance falls billions short of their reputations. Their brands act as false indicators.

Perhaps there is an explanation. Companies looking to go public are relatively small ones eager for the public offering that will generate the cash to turn them into large companies. Perhaps there is a mismatch here: the mammoth banks and the five-hundred-person Blue Mongoose almost hidden in an industrial park in Sunnyvale, California. Huge banks are better able to manage the financial needs of huge corporations like them, the Procter & Gambles, Microsofts, and Coca-Colas.

So let's imagine a better match. If Coca-Cola wants to acquire Jamba Juice or Evian, should it choose one of these huge firms?

Again, the latest data says no. The four big banks do not perform demonstrably better at managing mergers and acquisitions. What they do well is convince us they should manage these transactions, because they are the biggest and best known, and presumably able to attract the best employees to manage both IPOs and M&As. The biggest banks are best at creating the expectation that they will be the best. And so we think they are.

Will examples like these cause Americans to reassess the meaning of brands? It's unlikely. That's because none of us has a reliable method for comparing banks—or running shoes, toothpastes, shampoos, conditioners, or hundreds of other products and services. We trust brands because we cannot devise a more reliable test.

As a test, go to a Target and find the cheapest-branded shampoo you can find: Pantene. Take it home, take it to your shower, and wash your hair.

Does your hair feel 80 percent less clean, shiny, and manageable?

To the contrary, it probably feels better. There's a compelling argument that Pantene causes fewer bad hair days than any shampoo you can find, including those costing eight times more. Ask the person who cuts and shampoos your hair some time; just preface it, "Please, tell me the truth. I won't tell anyone."

To each of us, reality rarely is what is, or what is really happening, at any given moment. It is what we think it is and often merely what we think it must be. The Wizard of Oz is all powerful not because he is—he's a little old wild-haired man behind a curtain—but because Dorothy and her friends have heard that he is. Paris is magically romantic not because it is but because of all the stories we have heard for years that tell us, "Paris is magically romantic." Southerners are friendly, Volvos are safe, Six Sigma is genius and virtually indispensable, Maytag washers are indestructible. Or are they?

With all that said—that most trends are not trends and that expectations continue their incredible influence over everything we experience—we turn to two events that deserve attention as we try to understand this new century.

III. WHY WEALTHY RUNNERS LIMP: THE NEW FRUGALISTAS

—

Ever playful, Americans in the summer of 1972 took to the streets. Pushed outside by the race that launched a thousand sports-medicine clinics—Frank Shorter's startling win in the 1972 Munich Olympic marathon—Americans became runners.

They quickly learned that although our ancestors had loped for miles to chase their food, we moderns are less well adapted to running. Within a month of Shorter's win, runners' conversations focused on tendonitis, plantar fasciitis, and other ailments that just months earlier would have sounded like Portuguese to them.

Running's boom had become medicine's blessing. America was limping. Why?

For years, the answer appeared obvious. Doctors gave almost every running injury a technical description, such as achilles tendonitis, and the general heading "overuse syndrome." Runners simply were running too far, too often, too fast.

To reduce the risk of these overuse injuries, experts suggested stretching. Their theory was that stretching loosened and warmed muscles and tendons, which made them less susceptible to injury. Partly because this advice seemed so logical, many runners heeded it. And kept limping.

The running-shoe companies saw an opportunity and responded with "biomechanically designed" shoes based on scientific studies of our feet and legs. Naturally, they charged more for these shoes, a premium runners were willing to pay to keep on their feet.

Now well into the twenty-first century, the sport continues to attract millions, and runners continue to limp—provided their doctor hasn't insisted that they quit running entirely.

Which brings us to another interesting story about conventional wisdom, expert wisdom, and the reasons we buy what we buy. It's the story of what causes these injuries.

Researchers recently broke down every potentially relevant variable about runners—their gender, age, height, weight, running surface, miles run per week, average running pace, athletic background. To everyone who knew that injuries were caused by overuse, the studies seemed unnecessary, like the infamous government study that spent months reaching its recommendation for improving bike safety: Add a third wheel.

But the researchers found that the obvious explanation was wrong: Overuse wasn't the cause. Kooks like this author, who once ran an average of seventeen miles a day, suffered no more injuries than those who ran that much a week.

Was it failure to stretch? More kooks like this author refused to stretch, figuring that a slow start to a run was warm-up enough. These impatient kooks were right. Stretching didn't hurt, the researchers found, but it didn't help, either.

Did gender have an influence? Are women the more-injured sex? No.

Surely then—*surely*—weight figured into the problem. Extra weight *must* cause more injuries. But again, an obvious cause isn't a cause at all. Being overweight may be unhealthy, but it doesn't contribute to injuries.

Running surfaces—were they the explanation? It seems logical that harder running surfaces would produce more injuries and that softer surfaces, such as the bark-chipped Pre's Trail in Eugene, Oregon, help reduce injuries. But neither is true.

At this point, it might seem that nothing causes injuries. They're idiopathic—ailments without clear causes.

But at long last, we discover that they're not idiopathic. The study found the real cause of running injuries: As Mars Blackmon (played by the film director Spike Lee) once said in a memorable Nike ad, "It's gotta be the shoes!"

It's the shoes! Of course! Minimally designed shoes with inadequate cushioning and little or no motion control result in more injuries than properly designed shoes!

No. But there is a direct, absolute, and proven correlation between running shoes and running injuries. It's this: *The more expensive the shoe, the more injuries the wearer suffers.*

A rebel faction of runners suspected this for years. Running over two thousand miles a year, their bodies and brains gathered plenty of data and made them think that these more-engineered and expensive shoes were hazardous. For many of these rebels, their Aha! moment came in 1979.

That was the year the German-based juggernaut Adidas introduced the ultimate injury-prevention shoe, the startling Adidas TRX. Adidas offered this garish black and yellow hulk after years of testing. Adidas decided that if they could completely stabilize a runner's heel, it would retard the foot's inclination to rock inward. By reducing that motion—this entire class of shoes was called motion control shoes—the shoe would reduce the injuries caused by the movement.

Desperate for any shoe that would keep them off rest, ice, and aspirin, many American runners bought TRXs. Out on the roads on the days that followed, these well-protected men and women could be spotted for blocks. It wasn't just the shoes' Street Sign Alert black and yellow colors that caught the eyes of passersby; it was their massiveness. A runner in TRXs appeared to be running on twin waffle irons.

This strange sight, however, lasted only a few months on America's roads. It happened because TRX buyers soon became patients; their knees ached like never before.

The failure of the TRX and the finding that the higher the price, the more hazardous the running shoe seems to lay waste to the common American wisdom "You get what you pay for." It suggests the possible foolishness of that woman who cooed to us that she spent more on her L'Oréal hair color because she was worth it. It reminds us that our expensive DVD player is worth less to us because we have to spend so much time not really learning how to use it.

We take price tags as quality signals. A bit more

is a bit better, a lot more is a lot better, and the only questions are "What can I afford" and "How important is this product to me?"

But is a lot more a lot better? Are running shoes a unique case? It's unlikely, particularly because of another phenomenon at work in America today: With age comes wisdom.

You see this in the parking lot of outlet stores today. Years ago, the lots of these stores were filled with affordably priced, smaller cars. Today, drive into an Opitz Outlet: Three Mercedes, two Lexuses, a BMW, and a Land Rover leave fewer spaces for humbler cars.

If these spotless luxury cars catch our eyes first, the second thing that surprises us is the crowd. It's 2:20 p.m. on a chilly Tuesday; it's not a shopping hour on a shopping day in shopping weather. Plus Opitz's frequent buyers know that Tuesday is the wrong day to shop because the next day, Wednesday, is new shipment day.

But it doesn't matter. Americans are learning that if you head off on a treasure hunt, it's treasure you will find: $167 rich brown leather Rockport boots, fit for a cool night on South Beach in Miami, for $48.

Those Beemers in that lot belong to the Boomers. Over their years, they've learned that everything they ever bought at Neiman Marcus or Macy's was overpriced, at least temporarily. They've learned that patience, at least in shopping, is a virtue.

Their big first lesson came with calculators over twenty years ago. One day they cost $300 and could do only math. In what seemed like weeks, they could get a calculator just for opening a new bank account, and the device could calculate Fibonacci sequences. Seeing that, Boomers realized that had they just waited on that calculator back then, they would have saved almost every penny they spent.

This is where we are now. Welcome to the Age of the Great Recession, the Frugalistas, and the Beemers in the Opitz lots. Much like the fellow who submits to his first diet and afterward realizes that he doesn't really need butter and whole milk, we are apt to bring the habits of the new frugality with us, but our love of the freedom that money brings and our passion for play suggests that we will consume again, just not quite as conspicuously. Conscious consumption seems more likely as we give a new twist to the old L'Oréal saw:

"I paid $119 dollars less for my boots. *I'm worth it.*"

IV. The Cycling Clown and Wandering Gorilla: Our National Attention Deficit

---

In this age of faster, how do we explain millions of Americans watching baseball games—for three hours?

How do we explain three hundred people listening to a speaker for two hours without averting their eyes? Their faces? They look completely engaged and content.

Why?

Because we so rarely experience these moments of single focus on a simple thing, and that feeling—our Zen-like moment of connection to one thing—delights us.

Consider our constant alternative: enduring the

siege of words and images. Watch CNN financial news, for example. We hear a dark-suited anchor-person talking quickly. We may notice sentences like "Dow drops on IBM earnings report" jogging across the bottom of the screen. At the top of the screen, we might notice abbreviations and numbers racing by with the current prices of the most active stocks. We spot the time in the upper-right-hand corner, the temperature in the left, and the list of upcoming stories on the right. We are viewing as multitasking.

Meanwhile, we're scanning our local newspaper and checking our voice mails while Norah Jones sings in the background and our daughter croons in the foreground, "Can you play with me now?"

After we're done, we go check golf on the CBS website. On just the portion that fits our screen, we see fifty-nine—*fifty-nine!*—different web links we can hit. To check scores for the Masters, we see two links to "Scoreboard." We wonder, is one scoreboard better than the other? What if we choose the bad one? We are besieged by information and bewildered by what to do.

What is the almost inevitable result? But of course. When did we first hear of attention-deficit disorder, and why was it not more than fifteen years ago? Was this because no one suffered ADD in 1980? Or had it just not reached epidemic proportions?

What caused the epidemic? Did our species suddenly start selecting for a gene that predisposes humans to deficient attention? Or did the world change and the cascades of images and words so overwhelm so many of us that ADD became not just a diagnosis but a description of our culture?

In a world of people who cannot concentrate, how do we get and keep their attention? We've suggested that nothing gets attention like surprise.

Surprises delight us, intrigue us, grab us by the necks. The Oscar Meyer Wienermobile parks outside our favorite local burger spot. Many of the diners leaving the restaurant squeal when they see it, and every diner asks a passerby to take his photo. We love a surprise.

But even surprises are having trouble surprising us in this new century, as a clown discovered recently.

Imagine this spectacle: A clown in full clown regalia rides a unicycle across our favorite college's campus. Thousands of passersby stop, and dozens laugh out loud. But the clown steers by dozens of students who, when asked later, "Did you see the clown?" answer, "What clown?"

This spectacle occurred at Western Washington University in 2009, where researchers hired a clown to unicycle across campus. Yes, many students noticed the clown and reacted as the researchers predicted. But dozens of other students said, "What clown?" How could they?

It was because when the clown pedaled by, these students were talking on their cell phones. They cannot talk and see at the same time? Isn't that worse than being the fall guy in our famous old slam, the guy who could not walk and chew gum at the same time?

The clown at Western Washington suggests that our brains can do only so much. If it's engaged in talking, it's not seeing; if it's busy reading, it's not hearing. We multitask, perhaps, but our brains do not and cannot.

We are texting, talking, and Tweeting; we are checking the Web, religiously checking our email, seeing who has called. The more of this we do, the less of everything else we notice.

The researchers call us victims of inattention blindness. We are lost in the inner space of our brains. Out in the real world, clowns pedal by us on unicycles, ads cry out to us from every surface.

But we are blind.

Writing in the November 9, 2009, *New Yorker* about the clown case, Nick Paumgarter reminded readers of a bizarre parallel case: the missing plane. Just two weeks earlier, two Northwest Airline pilots overshot Minneapolis, their destination, by 150 miles. Their explanation?

At the moment when they should have been landing, they were reading on their laptops the new flight-crew scheduling procedures. One can only wonder: What if their laptops were showing a Ford Bronco fleeing the Los Angeles police? Would they have realized their mistake over Honolulu?

These stories of the unicycling clown and the distracted pilots reinforce the lessons of a famous older test. Dr. Daniel Simon of the University of Illinois and Christopher Chabris of Harvard once asked subjects to watch films of a basketball game and to keep track of the number of passes thrown by one team. When the test was completed, the test subjects proved to be experts at counting. What they weren't, however, were experts at noticing.

Midway through the film, a woman wearing a gorilla suit walked though the middle of the players for nine seconds, even stopping to face the camera and thump her chest. And what happened? *Almost half of the viewers didn't notice.*

But we know why, don't we? The more we try to see and do, the less we notice. Trying to notice basketball passes, we miss chest-thumping gorillas.

As any marketer knows, labeling something makes it seem real. Combine that with our characteristic self-confidence, and it's easy to see that we've come to believe in multitasking. But we don't multitask; we multitry. We are trying to do more, but we are accomplishing, and noticing, less.

This case of the missed gorilla seems unusually ironic. That's because fifty years ago, the iconic ad man David Ogilvy decried the trend in advertising toward award-winning ads that merely surprised, or even shocked, the viewers. Ogilvy said that an ad must offer a compelling premise, and that anyway, getting people's attention was simple. "All you have to do is show a gorilla in a jock strap."

Ogilvy might have been right then, but that was then. Today, it's not just marketing messages that are cluttered. It's our desks, our phones, and the focal point of all marketing, our brains. They're jammed.

This is not the Information Age. It's the Inundation Age.

Attention blindness has become the disease of our century. It forces marketers into being so surprising than even the blind will notice their ads. But ten years from now, will even that kind of audacity work? And what will?

In 2007, HarperCollins spent $10,000 creating three risqué videos to promote Chad Kultgen's book *The Average American Male*. In just two weeks, one million people watched the videos, which seemed to show that classic push techniques, pushed through new media like YouTube, could produce startling returns. But what were those one million eyeballs worth?

A blip: HarperCollins *printed* just ten thousand copies of the book. There's no record that it sold them; it just printed them. Publishers regularly go into second, third, even thirtieth printings of books, which raises the question: Did those one million YouTube viewers translate into one more buyer of the book?

The marketers' problem isn't just that we suffer from attention blindness. It's that even when we notice, we do nothing. We notice a Coors ad and say we love it—and go buy a Miller Lite instead. As HarperCollins might ask, what are a million eyeballs worth?

They might ask the former dot-com executives who saturated the 2000 Super Bowl with so many commercials that the game is also known as the Dot-Com Super Bowl. Those twelve companies spent $80,000 per second trying to get our attention. What did they end up with? Pennies on their original dollars or, in the cases of Pets.com, Epidemic.com, Computer.com, and OurBeginning.com, nothing.

These ads outperformed the clown on the unicycle and the gorilla—they got our attention—but the start-ups didn't realize the problems that creates. The first time someone gets our attention, we take away two messages: that they exist and that and we've never heard of them before. They're new and unfamiliar, and we love the familiar.

It's not attention good marketers want; it's attention over time, and products and services that deserve people's attention because they appeal to what Americans—we childlike Americans who think with our eyes—love.

SUMMING UP

We've just looked into our heads, and we may find ourselves nearing this conclusion: We're out of our minds.

We could excuse our foolishness—Dick Clark insisting that the Beatles would never fly, for example, and NBA players insisting that Kobe can—by recognizing that most of what we call thinking isn't. During our decision making, the organ that processes our data sits on the sidelines while our feelings do the work. When our feelings reach their decision, they summon our brains to come in and draft the rationale, a task it does so well that it manages to convince us that it's right—*and* that it was in charge the whole time.

Rational or emotional, do we ever grow up? We fight age, trying to live the Dylan wish that we stay forever young. We still love to play. Apple, Cuisinart, and the Mini Cooper turn phones, blenders, and cars into toys, and we crave them. The marketer who wants to thrive today asks, "How can I make this playful?"

From birth, we love surprises. Pose us a riddle—name our search engine Yahoo! or Google, for example—and we need to know the answer. Add a surprise to something familiar to us—a computer shaped like an egg and colored like a grape—and we inch closer to the cash register with it in hand.

One of our first long words is "story," and for good reason; we crave stories. Our movies, our songs, our evening news, our favorite television program of all time—they all are stories. The best marketers find their stories and they follow the ancient motto of McCann-Erickson: "The Truth well told." Those who try to make it up suffer the backlash that comes from our contempt for anyone who tries to fool us.

We want to be a part. As David Riesman noted in his 1959 classic *The Lonely Crowd,* we are "other-directed." We obsess over polls and best-seller lists because they reveal what others are thinking. The founders of Facebook, Twitter, and MySpace knew how much we dread loneliness and crave the respect and company of others. Of the three, Facebook appears to be the one true social gathering spot that will survive because it's the most "a part of" medium. Sell a motorcycle, and you sell some motorcycles; sell a motorcycle club, and you sell far more.

Yet we want to be apart, too. Gold is good, platinum even better. Nike shoes are good; our very own Nike shoes—or a Toyota Scion, with all its accessories—are even better. Like Malcolm

Gladwell, the shrewd marketer realizes this and speaks not to all of us but to each one of us: "Where do *you* want to go today?"

We crave the familiar. Our ancestors survived because of that: They had to fear anything new—large men uttering an odd language, for example. It's a risk, then, to offer us something too new, as *Mary Tyler Moore* and *60 Minutes* learned, as magazines learn every time they introduce a new design, and as Tropicana learned when it changed its packaging too dramatically. So today's marketer knows the key: Be just familiar enough. Apple introduces the Shuffle and flourishes because it feels familiar: We understand on-off and volume switches.

Our preference for the familiar suggests that brands will dominate this century, just as they did the previous one. We're all the Chicagoans who want their Marshall Field's, even if it's actually a Macy's, to be a Marshall Field's; we want what we know. Because we are uniquely impatient and have less time to choose among more products to choose from, brands represent simple, fast, and safe choices—and we crave simple, fast, and safe.

But new brands will emerge, and quickly if they give us what we love most: a unique and satisfying experience. It's happening already, of course: Facebook and Twitter are just two examples of services so new and attractive that they became forceful brands in months. That's today's Killer Brand: the unique, and uniquely satisfying, product.

We experience the world through our senses, particularly our eyes; we think with them. From childhood, we learn that beautiful is good for us; spots, rough edges, and discolorations are all signals of danger, and smooth is safe. Beauty tricks us from our childhoods, casting a halo that makes us give scholarships to football players who use Power-Point. Colors change us, too; they make hockey teams play more aggressively or make hockey referees more biased against teams in black—or perhaps they do both.

We shape things and then they shape us; we unclutter a neighborhood, and traffic fatalities soon drop dramatically. Design is a force, and it will grow as our products continue to mature and our choices grow in number; design breaks ties among our choices, and our world overflows with choices. Design has become the great value-added feature; we think with our eyes.

We love beauty, and nothing looks more beautiful to us than something simple. Today we will take twenty minutes to figure out a product. If we're still confused, we're driving back to the store with the receipt; we haven't got time for the pain. Simple is the new beautiful; complicated is the new defective.

But of all forces, none surpasses reputation. Reputations do not merely seduce us into choosing things; reputations change our experiences. If we think a concoction will sprout hair, for example, we soon see hair. Reputations also make us laugh when a humorist mourns the death of an old friend, make us prefer Coke when our taste buds adore Pepsi, and make our feet throb when we think six-inch nails are sticking through them. Reputations create our expectations, and our expectations change our perceptions.

We see that few trends are trends; most are fads that start to decline almost from the second we spot them. Fads come and go, and marketers eager to endure look beyond them and ask the question at the heart of this book: What leads us to choose what we choose?

This book has been my attempt to understand that better, by peeking into the most complex force in the universe: our minds. A few readers might disagree, arguing that physicists face more puzzling questions every day. They don't. Ask a few Ph.D.s in physics, and eventually you will learn something startling: The possible interactions of neurons in our brains outnumber all the particles in our universe.

So speaking of surprises, *just think about that*.

For the last fourteen years, I have argued that Marketing's goal is to reduce an enterprise's sales and advertising costs toward zero; to perform so well at the five must-dos—conceiving, designing, positioning, naming, and packaging—that little else is needed. If we learn later that we must do more—that we need to push—our problem isn't with our media or message; it's with our product.

And our solution isn't Twittering, Facebooking, or any form of "engaging the customer" that doesn't enhance peoples' experience. It's creating what people love. It's ingenious products like the Adidas micoach shoe, which makes the shoe more service—a coaching, training, and record-keeping service—than shoe; and the equally clever Polyvore website, which lets visitors mix and match clothes and accessories from twenty different store websites and share their concoctions and thoughts with the six-million-and-growing Polyvore fashion community.

This book has tried to find some patterns in our fascinating complexity and share them with you. If it has done nothing else, I hope this book has thumped you on your head a few times. It certainly has me; it's made me think, made me wonder, and made me smile.

If it has done that to you, too, that's all I could hope for—except to say thank you, and my best to you,

Harry Beckwith

The Unthinking Marketer's Checklist

Thinking About Kobe: Shortcutting and Stereotyping

What assumptions do your prospects likely make about your company, your product, your service, or you?

How can you take advantage of their positive assumptions?

What can you do to overcome their negative assumptions?

Big Versus Little

Is there a risk that you appear too big for some of your prospects, leading them to fear being treated as unimportant?

Similarly, can you reposition your larger competitors as being a risk for your prospects?

If you are a small company, are you leveraging the advantages of the underdog: an eagerness to serve and the tendency of underdogs to be more innovative?

Play

Do your website, promotions, and other marketing elements exploit the opportunities for offering viewers play—quizzes, contests, puzzles?

Do your products and services appropriately address our love of play?

Are you too serious?

The Power of Surprise

Do you have a $180,000 diamond in your marketing arsenal?

Are you surprising your customers and prospects?

Is your website surprising? Your storefront, office, and/or lobby?

Do your messages have an element of surprise that engages a reader?

The Power of Stories

Have you discovered your best stories?

Are your presentations story-based?

Are you telling your stories well?

Are your stories authentic and honest?

Do they resonate emotionally?

Do they develop dramatic tension, then surprise the reader with the outcome?

Our Obsession with Fairness

Are your customers convinced that your offerings and prices are fair?

Are they convinced that you and all your services are, too?

Our Preference for the Familiar

When you introduce something new, are you careful to make sure it is just familiar enough?

Are you making your brands and product names familiar to your most important prospects?

Freedom and Individualism

Have you "NikeiD-ed" your offering: Are your customers able to modify and customize your offering?

Our Need to Be a Part

Do you have your own Harley Owners Group: Have you considered ways of bringing customers into a community of users—of making them "a part"?

The Importance of Me

Do you address your prospects as individuals in all of your messages, or are your messages about your company and product instead?

Are you certain you are doing what you must to make sure your valued clients and customers feel truly important to you?

What tools and services can you create to make your most important and profitable customers feel special?

Are you hiring for your key customer-contact positions people who make others feel important? Are you particularly careful to hire good listeners?

The Importance of Just New Enough

Are your products and services just new enough, or are they like the Twinkies package, which had gotten too old?

Are you regularly updating your website?

Simplicity

Is what you are offering easy to understand, choose, order, and buy?

How can every step of the buying process be made faster?

Is your design simple and beautiful? (Buckminster Fuller once said he never thought about beauty as designing something, but that if his solution was not beautiful, he knew it was wrong.)

Does every element of the product or design matter?

Is it utterly clear how it works? (Note to makers of shower faucets: Could you agree on this somehow, so we don't waste minutes a year in hotel showers trying to figure out how to make the water warmer or cooler?)

Clarity and Cognitive Fluency

Are your name, message, customer interface, website, system, process, and instructions cognitively fluent—remarkably easy to understand, pronounce, access, and use?

Is it not just understandable but incapable of being misunderstood?

The Influence of Shapes and Colors

Are you certain that the shapes and colors you use convey the right message and mood? (For guidance, we recommend *Color Image Scale* by Shigenobu Kobayashi as a useful color guide.)

What do your colors convey?

What do they fail to convey?

Appealing to Feeling

Does your message appeal strongly to the emotions, or is it merely rational?

Have you identified the emotional forces that drive people to your products and those that might drive them away?

Do you know the emotional forces that drive people to choose your competitors?

How can you address and counter them?

Optimism

Is your message presented optimistically?

Is it focused on achieving good outcomes rather than on avoiding bad ones?

Conquering Our Attention-Deficit Disorder

Are you communicating so vividly that even people talking on their cell phones will notice, or are you too easy to overlook when other stimuli reach your prospective purchasers?

Are you making sure you get not just attention but the sustained attention that makes you familiar to prospects so they are comfortable with choosing you?

Are you getting attention in an honest and authentic way?

The Dominant Force of Expectations

Do you create the expectation that your product or service will be exceptional?

Are you using all your marketing channels to create the impression of excellence?

And are you managing all your processes to ensure that you regularly meet, and sometimes exceed, those expectations?

BIBLIOGRAPHY

Mustang: An American Classic, Mike Mueller

Iacocca, Lee Iacocca and William Novak

A Hard Day's Write, Steve Turner

Sundays with Sullivan, Bernie Ilson

Can't Buy Me Love: The Beatles, Britain, and America, Jonathan Gould

Let It Bleed: The Rolling Stones, Altamont and the End of the Sixties, Ethan A. Russell

Like a Rolling Stone: Bob Dylan at the Crossroads, Greil Marcus

American Gothic: The Biography of Grant Wood's American Masterpiece, Thomas Hoving

Out of Nowhere: The Inside Story of How Nike Marketed the Culture of Running, Geoff Hollister

Just Do It: The Nike Spirit in the Corporate World, Donald Katz

Swoosh: The Unauthorized Story of Nike and the Men Who Played There, J. B. Strasser

Love Is All Around: The Making of the Mary Tyler Moore Show, Robert S. Alley, Irby B. Brown, and Grant A. Tinker

McDonald's: Behind the Arches, John F. Love

People of Plenty, David M. Potter

The Mind and Its Stories: Narrative Universals and Human Emotion, Patrick Colm Hogan

On the Origin of Stories, Brian Boyd

This Is Your Brain on Music, Daniel J. Levitin

The Substance of Style, Virginia Postrel

The Art Instinct: Beauty, Pleasure, and Human Evolution, Denis Dutton

Survival of the Prettiest, Nancy Etcoff
The Creators, Daniel J. Boorstin
Decision Traps, J. Edward Russo and Paul J. H. Schoemaker
Uncertainty, David Lindley
More Than You Know, Michael J. Mauboussin
Think Twice: Harnessing the Power of Counterintuition, Michael J. Maboussin
The Paradox of Choice, Barry Schwartz
Predictably Irrational, Dan Ariely
How We Decide, Jonah Lehrer
How We Know What Isn't So, Thomas Gilovich
Homo Ludens, Johan Huizinga
The Courtier, Baldassare Castiglione
Candide, Voltaire
The Great Gatsby, F. Scott Fitzgerald
The Pursuit of Loneliness, Philip Slater
The Culture of Narcissism, Christopher Lasch
The American Mind, Henry Steele Commager
The Americans: The National Experience, Daniel Boorstin
The Americans: The Democratic Experience, Daniel Boorstin
The Image, Daniel Boorstin
Maslow on Management, Abraham Maslow
The New Brain, Richard Restak
Civilization and Its Discontents, Sigmund Freud
The Lonely Crowd, David Riesman
Loneliness: Human Nature and the Need for Social Connection, John T. Cacioppo and William Patrick
Bowling Alone, Robert Putnam
Stumbling Into Happiness, Daniel Gilbert
Hard Facts, Dangerous Half-Truths and Total Nonsense, Jeffrey Pfeffer and Robert I. Sutton
The Knowing-Doing Gap, Jeffrey Pfeffer and Robert I. Sutton
Influence, Robert B. Cialdini
The Marketing Imagination, Theodore Levitt

The Wisdom of Crowds, James Surowiecki

Outliers, Malcolm Gladwell

Blink, Malcolm Gladwell

Historians' Fallacies: Toward a Logic of Historical Thought, David Hackett Fischer

Remembering Denny, Calvin Trillin

The White Album, Joan Didion

Slouching Towards Bethlehem, Joan Didion

Trust, Francis Fukuyama

Traffic, Tom Vanderbilt

"The Unicycling Clown Phenomenon: Talking, Walking, and Driving With Cell Phone Users," Ira E. Hyman, *Applied Cognitive Psychology* 24 (9), December 2009.

"If It's Hard to Read, It's Hard to Do," Hyunjin Song and Norbert Schwarz, *Psychological Science* 19 (10), May 2008, 987–988.

"The Dark Side of Self- and Social Perception: Black Uniforms and Aggression in Professional Sports," Mark G. Frank and Thomas Gilovich, *Journal of Personality and Social Psychology* 54(1), January 1988, 74–85.

"Predicting Short-Term Stock Fluctuations by Using Processing Fluency," Adam Alter and Daniel Oppenheimer, *Proceedings of the National Academy of Sciences of the United States of America* 103(24), June 13, 2006, 9369–9372.

"The Keats Heuristic: Rhyme as Reason in Aphorism Interpretation," Matthew McGlone and Jessica Tofighbakhsh, *Poetics* 26(4), May 1999, 235–244.

"Red Enhances Human Performance In Contests," Russell A. Hill and Robert A. Barton, *Nature* 435(293), May 19, 2005, 1226–1229.

"Blue or Red? Exploring the Effect of Color on Cognitive Task Performances," Ravi Mehta and Rui (Juliet) Zhu, *Science* 27 323(5918), February 27, 2009, 1226–1229.

"The Bidder's Curse," Young Han Lee and Ulrike Malmendier, NBER Working Paper No. W13699, December 2007.

"Prospect Theory: An Analysis of Decision under Risk," Daniel Kahneman and Amos Tversky, *Econometrica* 47(2), March 1979, 263–291.

"You Are How You Eat: Fast Food and Impatience," Chen-Bo Zhong and Sanford E. DeVoe, *Psychological Science* 21(5), May 2010, 619–622.

"Mind-Set Matters: Exercise and the Placebo Effect," Alia Crum and Ellen Langer, *Psychological Science* 18(2), February 2007, 165–171.

For video of the "gorilla in the basketball game" experiment, see http://viscog.beckman.uiuc.edu/grafs/demos/15.html

For the footage of Stuart Brown's presentation on play and the polar bear and husky encounter, see www.ted.com/talks/stuart_brown_says_play_is_more_than_fun_it_s_vital.html

For added insight into the counterintuitive idea that trying to scare us into doing something—fastening our seat belts or stopping smoking, for example—can actually stimulate us to engage in that hazardous activity, see "When Scary Messages Backfire: Influence of Dispositional Cognitive Avoidance on the Effectiveness of Threat Communications," Steffen Nestler and Boris Egloff, *Journal of Research in Personality* 44(1), February 2010, 137–141.

Science Daily: Consumer Behavior News
www.sciencedaily.com/news/mind_brain/consumer_behavior/
Best summary of current consumer research.

Predictably Irrational.com, Dan Ariely
http://predictablyirrational.com

Useful resource from the author of a book by the same name.

The Frontal Cortex, Jonah Lehrer
http://scienceblogs.com/cortex/2007/03/a_science_of
_medical_performan.php
Ruminations of a bright new thinker.

Metafilter
www.metafilter.com
Outstanding trend-spotting source from thousands of non-mainstream stories.

PsyBlog
www.spring.org.uk/
Exceptional source on psychology based in the UK.

Mind Hacks
http://mindhacks.com/
Excellent source on psychology and the workings of the human brain.

Arts and Letters Daily
aldaily.com
The creation of Denis Dutton, a philosophy professor from New Zealand and author of *The Art Instinct*, a site maintained by the *Chronicle of Higher Education* and widely regarded as the Internet's best source for culture and ideas. Named the world's best website by the *Observer*. Added bonus: the best teaser headlines in journalism.

Reveries.com
The valuable brainchild of Tim Manners, author of *Relevance*. An excellent daily summary of news in marketing,

drawing on the *New York Times, Wall Street Journal*, and other leading sources, with a special focus on retail and shopper marketing.

The New York Times, 2003–2009 and select older issues
Business Week, 1994–2009 and select older issues
The Wall Street Journal, 2003–2009
Fortune, 1994–2009 and select older issues
Business 2.0, 1995–2009 and select older issues
Inc., 1992–2009 and select older issues
The Economist, select topics
The New Yorker, select issues
Vanity Fair, select issues
Rolling Stone, select issues
Billboard, select issues

ACKNOWLEDGMENTS

One muggy August afternoon in 1987, three months after my son Will was born, a TV reporter stopped me at an intersection of 11th and Nicollet in downtown Minneapolis.

"What do you think giving birth would be like?" he asked.

His timing was perfect.

At that moment I pictured Will's mother, Valerie, during labor, flashing looks at me that looked not just pained but homicidal. Fortunately, her anesthesiologist saved us both by injecting Val with huge doses of morphine.

So until now, whenever I recalled my favorite book acknowledgment, in which James Simon Kunen compared writing a book to having a baby— "Both bring something new into the world, and both are a pain in the a—"—I'd always thought, "That's clever, but writing a book doesn't make you hurt all over." That was until now.

I used to run 110 miles a week; that was easier. After edit eighteen on this book, I stopped counting. The table of contents may be the most edited in publishing history. I changed a single verb in the Beatles story six times; I beat up that poor word so many times that I started to fear it might retaliate.

Fortunately, many people helped on the birth of this one.

Rick Wolff, Leila Porteous, and everyone else at Hachette have praised, paid, and waited patiently throughout our sixteen-year partnership; L&B McCree and Bernadette Evangelist always make my ideas look better; Kristen Azzara and Bob Castillo fixed everything else.

Stanford's David Potter's ovation-provoking course on the American character inspired this book, and my other teachers—Theodor Geisel, John McPhee, Kurt Vonnegut, Jr., David Kennedy, Paul Robinson, James Robinson, Robert Horn, Cliff Rowe, William Zinsser, and William Clebsch—still influence me. I'd never have met most of those men were it not for Fred Hargadon and his admissions staff at Stanford, who in 1969 placed a wild bet on an underachiever from an Oregon town of sixty-five people. Thank you, everyone.

Larry Espel introduced me to Thomas Gilovich, whose work changed how I think, what I write, and what I advise.

Anyone who writes a book like this must be under some spell of Dr. Ellen J. Langer, who one day might be remembered as the pioneer of the great revolution of this century: how we think about ourselves.

The editors of *Science Daily, Arts & Letters,* and *Reveries* nicely summarize news in psychology, culture, and consumer behavior and gave me several ideas.

Twenty-two years ago my first editor, Steve Kaplan, advised me, "Tell stories." Every time I thank him for that, Steve acts as if it never happened. It did, Steve.

Years later, Malcolm Gladwell demonstrated that I needn't rush those stories, a lesson that helped me discover even more.

Three men have been special inspirations: Roger McGuinn, best known for leading The Byrds; John Lloyd Young, the Tony Award–winning actor in *Jersey Boys*; and Brandon Flowers of The Killers.

My father Harry and mother Alice promised my life would turn out nicely if I listened to them. Before they died—Dad much too young, mom four months before I began this manuscript—I hoped they realized they were right and that I was grateful. I still am.

Will, Harry, Cole, and Cooper always asked, "How's the book going?" and give me the spirit that infuses my books at their sunniest.

My remarkable sister Becky and her husband Jim—a delightful marriage of art and science—and brother David look smarter to me every week.

Neroli Lacey, Pam Haros, and Ty Votaw always listen hard and speak gently and provided valuable feedback. Thanks to you, too, Tyler Pace.

Laura, Kevin, Chirsty, Jim, Alex, Rachelle, and Auri of Burger Jones; Jen, Luke, Brianna, Eddie, Abby, Stevie, Shauna, Merrit, Kryn, and Kate at Caribou Coffee. Thanks for not charging rent for the tables.

I am indebted and grateful to Jason Damberg and Suzanne Remington, for reasons they know well.

Peter Glanville, Jim Stein, Jim Rockwell, Tim Klein, Molly Gillin, and Stephanie Prem, all of Lowry Hill, I've loved our ride.

As always, thank you Cliff Greene—and Kim, too.

Midway through this book's creation, The Duke and his saintly companion introduced me to their faith. Later on those Sunday nights and many others, we sat under bright moons that lit up their cobbled steps while we kept alive the world's cigar, gin, and wine industries and talked until we were drowsy. On my last day, I will remember those nights.

If the Olympics ever adds Tandem Laughing, Kevin McGregor and I will one day stand atop the medal stand as the "Star-Spangled Banner" plays. Its final notes will prompt tears down my cheeks, and Kevin to lean over and whisper something about a blonde in the second row. Everyone needs a Kevin McGregor, but decades on earth convince me: There's only one.

On December 13, 2009, Rita Lundgren, who had lived for twenty-one years in my snapshot memory of her, reappeared. By Christmas Eve I learned that she has a gift like my sister's, a painter's gift for seeing. Although she arrived late, Rita gave wise advice, and her spirit jumped right in here. You can hear it in my introduction and summary and are hearing it now.

All my life, I've been blessed to have lived among gifted people like Kevin and Rita. My mother's cooking attracted praise from the legendary chef James Beard, and my father Harry eliminated any need in our home for encyclopedias. Of three Rhodes Scholar friends, my best friend John Tillman, by his legendary freshman feat of writing a twenty-two-page research paper on the Albigensian Crusade entirely from memory, showed me that I needed to work much harder, particularly after my humbling afternoon two weeks later when I saw his professor's note on the paper: "With minor revisions, this could be the seminal work on the subject." Several friends inspired me by winning national championships and Olympic medals, which today are buried in their sock drawers because those medals are merely among their many accomplishments.

The last of these women and men became widely known for their gifts, but everyone listed here has a gift that he or she shared with me. I am incredibly grateful—damp-eyed as I write this. You make me know how lucky I am.

INDEX

About the Author

HARRY BECKWITH has advised companies around the world, including Target, Microsoft, and twenty-two other Fortune 200 companies, focusing on marketing and consumer behavior, and has won the American Marketing Association's highest award.

His previous books are required in business schools worldwide, have sold over 900,000 copies in twenty-four translations, and have been *New York Times, Wall Street Journal*, and *Business Week* best-sellers. *Selling the Invisible* appears on numerous "best business books of all time" lists.

Harry is an award-winning lecturer and speaker, having addressed graduate business schools including Stanford, Wharton, Chicago, NYU Stern, Carlson, Technologio de Monterrey (Mexico), and Amity (Delhi, India), and companies and groups in twenty-one other countries.

His background in American history and culture traces to his undergraduate years at Stanford University, from which he graduated Phi Beta Kappa in history. He has written extensive papers on the Nuclear Test Ban Treaty of 1962, the evolution of

American entertainment forms, the 1765–1771 Regulator controversy in North Carolina, and the relationship between technology and American values, a senior thesis that was made part of permanent exhibit of the Ford Foundation.

He also has written documentaries on the wreck of the *Edmund Fitzgerald* for the Great Lakes Shipwreck Museum; on Hubert Humphrey's landmark speech on civil rights at the 1942 Democratic National Convention, for the Hubert Humphrey Museum; and on *Lost Twin Cities,* an acclaimed documentary produced for Minnesota Public Television. As a law clerk to a federal judge in 1976, after receiving his doctorate of jurisprudence degree and serving as editor-in-chief of the *Oregon Law Review,* he authored the U.S. District Court opinion for *Wilson vs. Chancellor,* still considered a major American case on freedom of speech.

As a careful reader of this book might suspect, he's also a former national-class marathoner (and cofounder of a famous road race, the Cascade Run Off) and former college disc jockey, as well as the writer of three pop—but not popular—songs.

He is the proud father of three sons—Harry IV, Walter William, and Cole—and a daughter Cooper; a member of the Stanford University Board of Athletic Advisors; and a participant in several initiatives aimed at improving American education.

Harry can be reached at beckwithpartners.com, read on Twitter, or emailed directly—at invisble@bitstream.net (please first notice the missing letter "i") or beckwithpartners.com. Please know that he returns emails—in English, Spanish, Hungarian, and Turkish—with a speed that has stunned correspondents from all over the world.

**BUSINESS
PLUS**

Recognized as one of the world's most prestigious business imprints, Business Plus specializes in publishing books that are on the cutting edge. Like you, to be successful we always strive to be ahead of the curve.

Business Plus titles encompass a wide range of books and interests—including important business management works, state-of-the-art personal financial advice, noteworthy narrative accounts, the latest in sales and marketing advice, individualized career guidance, and autobiographies of the key business leaders of our time.

Our philosophy is that business is truly global in every way, and that today's business reader is looking for books that are both entertaining and educational. To find out more about what we're publishing, please check out the Business Plus blog at:

www.businessplusblog.com